Coin Collecting as a Hobby

REVISED EDITION

Burton Hobson

EDITED BY ROBERT OBOJSKI

Sterling Publishing Co., Inc.   New York

COIN & STAMP BOOKS

The author wishes to thank the American Numismatic Society, Q. David Bowers, the Trustees of the British Museum, the Cleveland Museum of Art, the Franklin Mint, the German National Museum of Nurnberg, the Medallic Art Co., the Royal Mint, B.A. Seaby, Ltd., and the Smithsonian Institution for their co-operation in supplying illustrations. The photographs of coining tools shown on pages 119, 122 and 123 are Crown copyright and are used by permission of the Controller of Her Majesty's Stationery Office.

CONTENTS

Why Collect Coins?

Old coins, and new ones too, have an attraction that most of us find hard to resist. Issues such as the U.S. Eisenhower dollar and Kennedy half dollar and the British Churchill crown are put away by the millions into drawers, boxes, purses and

Great Britain, 1981 crown—commemorates the marriage of H.R.H. the Prince of Wales (Prince Charles) to Lady Diana Spencer.

U.S., 1971 dollar—President Dwight Eisenhower memorial coin, Apollo 11 moon-landing team insignia on the reverse.

albums. Even before Britain adopted decimal coinage, the crown piece, like the American dollar, was not used in everyday commerce, so those coins were not even intended for circulation, but were specially minted as commemoratives for coin collectors and for those who wanted a memento of these great men.

Let an old coin turn up, a discontinued type dated fifty or a hundred years ago, and the reaction is the same. Not only is the coin put away for safekeeping but the finder immediately

Most coins found in circulation have recent dates, but in countries like the U.S. where the same size coins have been used for more than a century, older issues such as Indian Head cents do on rare occasions turn up in everyday change.

starts exhibiting it to his friends and making inquiries about its value. While many people make the mistake of equating old age with worth, it is true that coins have value—an intrinsic metal value, a face value, and, at least in most cases, an even greater value to collectors.

COIN VALUES

The element of value is the factor that appeals most to non-collectors. Everyone has heard stories of tremendous prices paid for old coins. It is a fact that an 1804 U.S. silver dollar sold for $150,000 in 1974, and five years later another specimen of this extremely rare dollar brought $225,000. At a July 1979 auction, a 1787 Brasher "Doubloon" fetched $430,000, a record for any single coin. In November of the same year, a different specimen brought $725,000 at auction. No coin has ever changed hands for a higher price. An ancient Greek silver dekadrachm struck in Sicily circa 425 B.C. brought $1,000,000 in a 1980 private sale, the highest price yet recorded.

This extremely rare U.S. 1787 Brasher "Doubloon" was hammered down for an astounding $725,000 at a November 1979 auction sale staged in New York City. This is the highest price ever paid at auction for a single coin. The storied gold piece, weighing some 408 grains, was produced by Ephraim Brasher, a New York goldsmith, to equal the value of a Spanish doubloon (about $16.00).

This rare 1825 Russian ruble of Czar Konstantine was sold at public auction on November 20, 1965 for $41,000, then a record-breaking price for a single coin.

Not only old coins, but even many coins of recent issue, have value. Some examples are the 1930 Australian penny ($15,000), the 1936 Canadian cent with a dot below the date ($5,000), the 1951 British penny (£20) and the U.S. 1955 cent with the double die obverse ($1,500).

While rare coins such as those listed above are in great demand and do bring high prices, the vast majority of coins sell for much less. A leading coin retailer in the United States recently computed that his average transaction was about $3.75 and recalled individual sales over the preceding year ranging from 10¢ to $6,000. More than half of the coins he

Australia,
1930 penny ($15,000)

U.S., 1955 cent — double
die obverse variety ($1,500)

Even some seemingly ordinary coins of recent issue can bring high prices because of the scarcity of certain dates or particular varieties. Many similar coins, however, are worth only their face value. Coin collectors must have sharp eyes indeed.

sold were priced at a dollar or less. Literally thousands of different coins can each be purchased for less than the price of a cinema ticket and the entertainment factor is infinitely more lasting!

Canada, 1958 dollar

This interesting coin with its totem pole reverse was widely available for a small premium during the year of issue.

Since coins, except for the relatively few that can be found in circulation, do cost something, one of the first things a potential collector wants to know is whether coins are wise purchases and what profit or loss he can expect on his investment. In one sense, and assuming that we are talking about moderately priced coins, most collectors feel that just the pleasure alone of owning an unusual coin repays its cost.

Supply and demand

Every coin has a market value, the price that dealers are currently charging for it. This price is determined by supply and demand—the available quantity of a coin and the number of collectors and degree of interest they have in owning it. If there are enough coins to go around, the price will be moderate, because coin dealers compete sharply for collectors' business. On the other hand, if a few coins have to be divided among many collectors, rivalry bids the price up quickly.

U.S., 1870-S half dime

This 1870 San Francisco Mint silver half dime, considered to be unique, was sold at a September 1985 auction in New York City for $176,000. The seller took an enormous loss, however, since he paid $425,000 for the coin at a 1980 private treaty transaction. Interestingly, the 1870-S half dime did not come to light until the early 1970s. Though there are no official U.S. Mint records of this particular half dime, a team of numismatic experts has certified the coin as being genuine.

If you ask a non-collector his opinion of what makes a coin valuable, he will answer unhesitatingly, "Rarity!" It is true that rarity is a large part of the answer, but it is not the whole answer.

Again in the eyes of a non-collector, the age of a coin is also a prime factor in determining value. This is true to some extent but again it is not the whole story. The coin trade has other standards besides age and rarity in assessing coin values.

The value of a given coin is a complex thing. The number of pieces struck during the year of issue naturally has much to do with it. As you would expect, an 1877 Indian Head cent with a mintage of fewer than one million pieces is worth about ten times as much as the older 1867 of which nearly ten million were made, and approximately 100 times as much as the 1887 with a coinage of 45 million pieces.

Low mintage alone, however, is not enough to make a coin valuable. A coin may be scarce, but if there is little or no demand for it, then it will not be valuable. Lack of demand leaves prices on a fairly even keel. Many of the world's coins and certainly most of the ancient coins are rare and the supply

This 1817 U.S. large cent would cost about $60 (£40) because of its fine state of preservation. The same coin in more worn condition, however, can be purchased for as little as $7.50 (£5).

is limited, to be sure. But the demand for them is nothing like the demand for certain coins of the U.S., Britain and other popularly collected countries, which is why these coins sell for several times the price of actually scarcer and older coins.

Another key element is the physical state of a coin—its condition. Coins in new, uncirculated condition—just as they left the mint—are obviously more attractive than worn or battered coins. They are so much more desirable, in fact, that coins in choice condition command substantial premiums over coins in average condition. A coin in brilliant, uncirculated condition can easily be worth ten times as much as the identical coin in used condition. On the other hand, mutilation or damage to a coin detracts from its value. Unless it is a rare date, a coin in poor condition is worth little or nothing to a collector.

This 1985 Falkland Islands 50-pence silver crown commemorates the opening of the new Mount Pleasant Airport (situated only a few miles from the capital of Stanley) by Prince Andrew on May 12, 1985. The coin's obverse bears the new effigy of Queen Elizabeth II, which was created by the noted engraver Raphael Maklouf.

Collectors have the "law" of supply and demand working for them. The supply of most coins is constantly decreasing as more and more coins go into collections, and demand is building as more and more people take up the hobby. Population growth and increasing leisure time alone should assure ever more collectors. Thus a collector may very likely find that after he has held on to a coin for a few years, its price will have gone up to the point where fifty per cent of the market value is more than his original purchase price. Coin collecting is one of the few hobbies one can enjoy over the years and still stand to make a profit. Profits are especially likely if a collector concentrates on coins that are readily available now, but are likely to gain more and more popularity with the passage of time.

The fascination of coins

What powerful fascination do coins have that collectors are willing to pay a premium price for them, to spend hours of their time searching for more coins, and arranging and learning about the coins already in their possession?

A great deal of excitement was created when the new Lincoln Memorial cent was first released in 1959. It was reported that the small "o" in "OF" was an error and that the coins were being recalled.

Stories about coins of special value being found in circulation or reports that errors in coinage have inadvertently been released by the mint have been responsible for the creation of many new collectors. When the cent with the new Lincoln Memorial reverse was first released in 1959, for example, collectors noticed that the name of the country was spelled out UNITED STATES OF AMERICA, all capital letters except for the small "o" in "of." Rumors soon spread that the engraver had made a mistake and all of the new coins would soon be recalled. Banks were besieged with demands for the new coins and were soon doling them out one to a customer if at all. Coin dealers and collectors were overwhelmed with requests for information.

As the government later explained, no error had been committed at all. The small "o" was purposely used to indicate that "of" was subordinate to the other three words in the legend and because the designer felt the introduction of the small letter made the legend artistically pleasing and more interesting to look at. The whole story was amusing to informed coin collectors who knew, of course, that the legend had appeared in this same fashion for the preceding eleven years on all of the Franklin half dollars.

The rumors were true, however, in the case of the 1955 double die cent shown on page 8 (enlarged photo on p. 133). This rare variety was not known until some specimens were found among everyday coins. Nearly all of the examples available were retrieved from circulation. Once you start looking for information about one coin, you are likely to find yourself caught up in a fascinating study.

If you have the least imagination, a coin of a foreign country seems to have the power to carry you there—not bodily, of course, but the knowledge that the coin in your hand passed from hand to hand in another land does create the feeling of close contact. Coins can do what no ship or aircraft or even rocket can do.

Coins such as this 50 franc piece from French Polynesia (Tahiti) with its tropical scene of palm trees, beach, native hut and outrigger canoe can start you dreaming of faraway places.

Austria,
1964 50 schillings

Bahamas,
1970 50 cents

Coins can take you ski jumping or deep-sea fishing as on these recent issues, one a commemorative, the other a regular circulation issue.

Collector or not, you will experience a genuine thrill when you actually look at a bit of silver or bronze and realize that it served people of a distant day or land just as the coins in your pocket serve you. Moreover, for the collector there is the excitement of the hunt. Identifying an unfamiliar coin or acquiring an elusive item for which you have searched far and wide produces a sense of accomplishment that is hard to match.

This coin from Western Samoa honoring Robert Louis Stevenson combines the lure of a far-away place with the name of a man familiar to all readers of English literature. Stevenson spent the last four years of his life in Samoa.

This silver testone of Florence with the portrait of Alexander di Medici (1533–36), dating from the Italian Renaissance, is believed to have been struck from dies engraved by Benvenuto Cellini, the famous goldsmith.

Coins as works of art

Apart from the fun of acquiring coins and the lure of history and distance that they represent, coins are attractive in themselves. They are often miniature works of art. In the case of ancient, medieval, and Renaissance coins, each one is an original work, hand-hammered from dies that were hand-cut by master craftsmen. As a matter of fact, many art museums feature coins in their displays.

These beautiful fourteenth-century gold coins (left) gold leopard of Edward the Black Prince of Aquitaine, 1355–75, and (right) gold mouton d'or of John the Good of France, 1350–64, are on exhibit at the Cleveland Museum of Art. The names of the coins come from the animals shown on them.

15

Mot:fs from ancient art are sometimes borrowed for modern coins as
on this 5 pound gold piece struck in Egypt in 1955.

While the prices of fine paintings and sculptures are such
that we must leave them to the museum galleries, enough
coins are available so that nearly everyone can afford to bring
some examples of coin art into his home. Visiting a museum
and seeing the rare coins in glass cases is an interesting and
informative experience, but it cannot be compared to the
pleasure of owning an old coin of your own, no matter how
modest, one that you can handle, carry about, study and
examine at your leisure. Happily, many, many coins are
available to private collectors.

Students of art will be interested in comparing these two versions of
St. George and the dragon. At left is the famous Pistrucci interpreta-
tion on a crown piece of 1818. The "modern" rendering at right
appeared in 1935.

Coin collecting as a hobby

Collecting coins as a pastime dates back at least to the days of the ancient Romans. We know from Roman historians that they prized Greek coins and their own antique issues. Pope Boniface VIII (1294–1303) and Petrarch (1304–74), the Italian poet, are known to have been coin collectors. In England, the Stuart monarchs beginning with James I (1603–25) were ardent collectors of coins. These first collectors limited their attention almost exclusively to the "classic" coins, those of the Greeks and Romans. Even as collectors turned their attention to coins of their own nations, it was the early issues that counted; contemporary coins were ignored.

Augustus   Nero

The earliest collectors were interested primarily in ancient coins. Their goal was often to represent each of the Roman emperors with a single coin such as these silver denarii of the first century A.D.

The goal of collecting was to acquire one coin of each of the Roman emperors or of each of the British monarchs. An extensive collection might include more than one specimen of the same reign, but certainly of a different denomination or design type.

Coin collecting in America got started on a different foot. The first known collector was Joseph Mickley of Philadelphia, who decided in 1817 that he would like to have a fine specimen of a large cent dated 1799, the year of his birth. As it happened, 1799 was the rarest date of the large cents, and by the time he found the coin he wanted, he had assembled quite a collection. As the first U.S. coins had been struck in 1793,

17

The early collectors of U.S. coins wanted a coin of every different date even though the design was the same. The large cents such as the 1808–14 turban head of Liberty design were especially popular and much sought after. The tradition of collecting the various periods by dates has continued and is by far the most popular kind of collecting in America today.

there weren't many "old coins" to collect in 1817. Mickley and his friends went on to collect the other denominations by date, thus establishing in America a tradition of collecting all dates of a series rather than one of a type, as was until recently more often the case in Europe.

Mexico, 1953 5 centavos (denomination first issued in 1863)

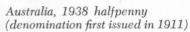

Australia, 1938 halfpenny (denomination first issued in 1911)

New Zealand, 1953 halfpenny (denomination first issued in 1940)

The idea of collecting series of coins by date has spread to Britain, Canada, Mexico, Australia, New Zealand—in fact, to nearly every country with regular annual coinages.

Germany, 1951 5 marks. Modern German coins offer a challenge to collectors since, like U.S. coins, they are struck at various mints as well as with annually changing dates. The mint mark on this type is on the reverse below the date (G = Karlsruhe). Others are D = Munich, F = Stuttgart and J = Hamburg.

Getting Started in
Coin Collecting

THE BEST KIND of collection, obviously, is the kind that pleases *you* most. Before you can decide what kind appeals to you most, you have to know what the possibilities are. The following pages present a survey of the different approaches to coin collecting and explain what is involved in each. Bear in mind that there is no "one way" or even "best way" to

Book-type coin albums combine the finest features for display and protection of coins with ease of storage. Many albums are imprinted at each opening for the coin intended for that space—with the date, mint mark and quantity issued.

collect. Any one of these basic plans can and should be adapted to suit your own taste and interest.

SERIES COLLECTING

The goal of series collectors is to complete a set of a given series of coins—such as U.S. Lincoln Head cents, Canadian small cents, British farthings, or Mexican centavos. This method is usually popular for collecting current or recently issued coins, especially when every mint mark and design variety is counted as a different coin.

Coins from circulation

Collectors everywhere are likely to start this way with coins of their own countries, because they can find coins in their day-to-day pocket change. The lower-denomination coins receive the most attention because the face-value investment is the lowest and because everyone handles more of them every day.

There is no reason, of course, why you cannot collect more than one denomination at the same time. A good plan, however, is to concentrate on one series first. If an older date coin of another denomination comes along, hold on to it for later but at the moment give your main attention to one series. For the first weeks of your collecting, you will probably discover at least one coin a day. As your collection fills out, however, it will become more difficult to find dates that you need and things will slow down a bit. When this happens, switch your attention to the next collection, but keep watching for the dates needed to complete that first set.

When you are ready to start on your collection, the very first thing is to begin checking the coins that pass through your hands each day. To do this efficiently, be sure to have a separate pocket or purse where you can put each coin given you during the day. Check your pocket coins as soon as possible against your collection and any coins not wanted can be put back in your regular change pocket to be given out again the next day. The secret of finding coins with scarce

The two most popular series for U.S. beginners are Lincoln cents and Jefferson nickels. New collectors usually start with the lower denomination coins and work up to the higher. The pre-1964 silver-content dimes, quarters and half dollars, however, have completely disappeared from circulation.

dates in circulation is to be consistent. If you are watching your coins, watch all of them. If you only look at the date when you "think it might be a good one," you are bound to let most of the scarcer ones slip right by.

When you are ready to check coins against your collection, sit down near a strong light. Pick up one of the coins to be checked and read the date and mint mark. Turn to your check list or the space provided in your album for that particular coin. If the space is empty, you have made a "find" and you place the coin in it. If the space is filled, compare the condition of the new coin with the one already there and retain the better of the two pieces.

You may wish to search through more coins than come your way in daily change. It is possible to purchase rolls of coins from banks and you may also be able to arrange to go through

Britain, Australia and New Zealand have all recently adopted decimal coins. In Britain, the old 1 shilling piece (left) is equivalent to 5 new pence (right). In Australia and New Zealand, the shilling has become 10 cents. This switch in coinage has limited the possibilities for collecting from circulation in these countries but many of the old coins are still readily available.

GEORGE VI

1937   1938   1939   1940

1941   1942   1943   1944

1945   1946   1947   1948

1949   1950   1951   1952

ELIZABETH II

1953   1954   1955   1956

Complete date set of farthings of the reigns of George VI and
Elizabeth II arranged as they appear displayed in coin albums.

23

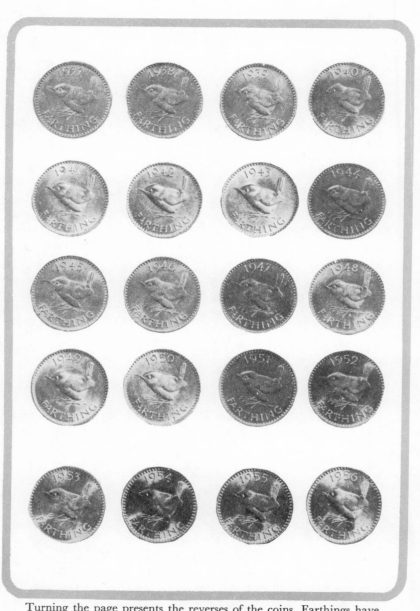

Turning the page presents the reverses of the coins. Farthings have now been withdrawn from use in England.

coins taken in at local stores, from parking meters, vending machines, collection plates, etc.

A few duplicates of each issue can be saved for trading stock although it is pointless to save too many of any one issue. For instance, if you are able to find 25 or 50 pieces of the same item, you can be sure that any potential trader you meet will have found at least the one specimen of that issue needed for his own set.

If you do save duplicates, remember always to save the ones in best condition. Some collectors like to work on a "second set" of each series which they keep exclusively for "trade bait." If you are fortunate enough to find extras of any of the really scarce dates, you can easily sell them to a coin dealer at a good price.

In nearly every series of coins, certain dates are scarcer than others. The English pennies of George VI provide a good example of this. The usual quantity minted of the dates between 1937 and 1948 was in excess of 50 million pieces of each issue. Coinage dropped off to 14 million in 1949, plunged to 240,000 in 1950 and only 120,000 in 1951. Consequently, while the earlier George VI pennies (none coined in 1941, 1942, or 1943) can still be easily found in circulation, the 1949 date requires more patience or good luck and it is virtually impossible to find a 1950 or 1951. In fact, these now sell for a premium of about £15 ($22.50) and £20 ($30) respectively, depending upon condition.

For series collectors, Canada offers small cents dated from 1920 to the present. The majority of dates can still be easily found in circulation. Since 1908, all Canadian coins have been struck at one mint, the Royal Canadian Mint in Ottawa, all without mint marks. Two varieties of 1947 Canadian cents were issued, some with a small maple leaf following the date. Both varieties should be included in a series collection. Also a "dot" variety of the 1936 cent exists, marking coins actually struck in 1937 from the previous year's dies. The dot variety

Canada, 1947 cents — regular issue and variety with small maple
leaf after date, indicating use of the die during 1948.

is extremely rare, however, with about five specimens known,
so collectors consider their sets complete without it.

In the United States, date and mint-mark sets of the Lincoln
Head cent series have been by far the most popular. From
1909 until 1955 these coins were issued in most years from three
different mints ("D" for Denver, "S" for San Francisco, no
mint mark for Philadelphia). Separate Philadelphia and Denver
issues continued until 1965 when the "D" mint mark was
discontinued. In 1968 Denver resumed issuing its coins with
mint marks, while the San Francisco mint reopened in 1968,
and the "S" mint mark returned.

Coins struck at Philadelphia have generally not carried
mint marks. However, since 1980, all coins produced at
Philadelphia, with the exception of the one cent piece, have
been inscribed with the "P" mint mark.

Location of mint marks on U.S. coins

Indian Head Cents: on the reverse, under the wreath.
Lincoln Head Cents: on the obverse, under the date.
Silver Three Cents: on the reverse, to the right of the "III."
Liberty Head Nickels: on the reverse, to the left of "cents."
Buffalo Nickels: on the reverse, under "Five cents."
Jefferson Nickels: on the reverse, to the right of the building,
    or above it; on the obverse, beside the date after 1967.
Liberty Seated Half Dimes: on the reverse, within or under the
    wreath.

1947   1947-D   1947-S

Series collections of U.S. coins include all date and mint-mark varieties. The two coins at the right show "D" and "S" mint marks at the right of the building. Coins of the same date but different mints are considered distinct varieties.

Liberty Seated Dimes: on the reverse, within or under the wreath.

Liberty Head Dimes: on the reverse, under the wreath.

Mercury Head Dimes: on the reverse, to the left of the fasces.

Roosevelt Dimes: on the reverse, at the left bottom of the torch; on the obverse above the date after 1967.

Twenty-cent Pieces: on the reverse, under the eagle.

Liberty Seated Quarters: on the reverse, under the eagle.

Liberty Head Quarters: on the reverse, under the eagle.

Standing Liberty Quarters: on the obverse, above and to the left of the date.

Washington Quarters: on the reverse, under the eagle; on the obverse at the back of the neck after 1967.

Liberty Head Half Dollars: on the reverse, under the eagle.

Walking Liberty Half Dollars: on the obverse, below "In God We Trust," or on the reverse, below branch at lower left.

Franklin Half Dollars: on the reverse, above the Liberty Bell.

Kennedy Half Dollars: on the reverse, below the olive branch; on the obverse, below the neck after 1967.

Liberty Head Dollars: on the reverse, under the eagle.

Peace Dollars: on the reverse, at the bottom, to the left of the eagle's wing.

Eisenhower Dollars: on the obverse, above the date.

Susan B. Anthony Dollars: on the obverse, at the left of the neck.

Building your collection

In forming a collection of coins from circulation, there are two things that you must try to do. The first is to find one coin of each different date, from each different mint. Your second goal must be to find the coins in the best possible condition. Superior-condition coins are certainly more pleasing to own and display. The finer they are, the more desirable, and hence more likely to become valuable in the future.

Condition—how well a coin is preserved or how badly it is worn—has a great deal to do with its value. Collectors set great store by condition and like to get coins in the best possible condition. When you are buying coins, you will find that the

The well-worn (good condition) 1909 VDB cent at the left sells for about $3.00, the uncirculated specimen at the right for about $15.00. The difference in value is due entirely to the condition of the specimens.

asking price for a superior condition specimen can run ten or more times as much as for exactly the same coin in poor condition. Some collectors are almost fanatical in regard to condition, demanding and accepting coins only in the very best state of preservation. Such coins command a heavy premium, but these perfectionist collectors are satisfied to have fewer coins as long as they are in top condition. At the other extreme are collectors who will take coins in any condition as long as they are cheap. Most collectors buying coins fall somewhere in between. They want decent-looking, unmutilated coins with clear designs and legends, but are willing to take coins that show a moderate amount of wear. By accepting specimens in less than perfect condition, a collector can get many more coins for the same amount of

FDC
£6 ($9.00)

EF
£2 ($3.00)

FINE
40p ($.60)

VF
£1 ($1.50)

POOR
10p ($.15)

GOOD
20p ($.30)

The values of discontinued coin types also depend upon their condition. These British pennies shown with their approximate retail prices in Britain and the U.S. are all of equal rarity—the wide spread in price is due to the condition of the individual pieces.

money. Of course, a somewhat worn coin has actually been in use, and there is always the intriguing possibility that it may have been in famous hands or a witness to important scenes.

If you are collecting coins from circulation, you can continually try to improve on the condition of the coins in your collection. Your first goal is to find an example of every coin in the series, and your second goal should be to keep replacing coins when you come across one in better condition. Each design has one spot that shows wear first. This point is often crucial in judging which of two coins is in better condition. Superior-condition coins are more pleasing to own and display and are always more valuable. Of course, searching for better specimens, that is, upgrading the coins already in your collection, will give you just that much more opportunity to work with your coins. The challenge is greater and so is the feeling of accomplishment when the series finally measures up to a high standard.

If you are buying coins, you will want to get only coins in satisfactory condition right away. It usually works out best to buy the first time a coin that you will be happy with later.

CONDITION TERMS

In buying coins, especially by mail, you must understand the terms dealers and collectors use to describe the condition of coins. With this information, you will know what to expect (and what not to expect) if you buy a coin described as "fine." Since the price varies with the condition, you want to be sure to get as good a coin as you have paid for. On the other hand, you must not expect to get an "uncirculated" coin for the "very fine" price. Not surprisingly, in buying, selling, or trading coins there is often more dispute over the grading than the price. Grading is the process of assigning the proper label to a given coin.

The American Numismatic Association in the mid-1970s completed a standard grading system for coins based on a numerical scale from 1 to 70. The scale was originally devised by Dr. William H. Sheldon for his book *Penny Whimsy* (1958), and it has now been adapted for use with the entire United States series, thus providing uniform grading terminology. The Sheldon scale can also be easily utilized for grading most world coin issues.

According to Sheldon, the term "uncirculated," interchangeable with "mint state" (MS), refers to a coin which has never been circulated. A coin as bright as the time it was minted, or with very light natural toning, can be described as "brilliant uncirculated." A coin which has natural toning can be described as "toned uncirculated." Except in the instance of copper coins, the presence or absence of light toning does not affect an uncirculated coin's grade. Indeed, as Sheldon emphasizes, among silver coins, attractive natural toning often results in the coin bringing a premium. Moreover, because uncirculated coins may have slight imperfections, there are several subdivisions in that category within the Sheldon scale.

Here, in generalized terms, are the accepted standards for each condition:

PERFECT UNCIRCULATED (MS-70) — In perfect new condition. This is the finest quality available. Such a coin under four-power magnification shows no bag marks, lines, or other evidence of handling or contact with other coins. A brilliant coin can be described as "MS-70 brilliant" or "perfect brilliant uncirculated." An MS-70 brilliant is extremely rare, and many veteran dealers claim they've never seen one. In Europe, the absolutely perfect coin is usually referred to as FDC (Fleur de Coin).

CHOICE UNCIRCULATED (MS-65) — This refers to an above-average uncirculated coin which may be brilliant or toned (and described accordingly), and which has very few bag marks or rim marks. The MS-67 or MS-63 rating indicates a slightly higher or lower grade of preservation. In trying to pinpoint grades more exactly, numismatists now often use MS-67+ and MS-64 designations.

UNCIRCULATED (MS-60) — This is called "typical uncirculated" without any other adjectives. This designation refers to a coin which has a moderate number of bag marks on its surface. Also evident may be a few minor edge nicks and marks, although not of a serious nature. A coin may be either brilliant or toned. A true uncirculated coin has no trace of wear.

Canada, large cents, George V

Uncirculated

CHOICE ABOUT CIRCULATED (AU-55) — Only a small trace of wear is evident on the highest points of the coin. Most of the mint lustre remains.

ABOUT UNCIRCULATED (AU-50) — Traces of wear are visible on many of the high points of the design. Only half of the mint lustre is still present.

CHOICE EXTREMELY FINE (EF-45) — Light overall wear shows on all the highest points. All design details are clear and sharp. Mint lustre remains only in the protected areas of the coin's surface, such as between the star points and in the letter spaces.

EXTREMELY FINE (EF-40) — The design is lightly and evenly worn overall, but all features are quite sharp and well defined. Small traces of lustre may show.

Extremely fine   Very fine

CHOICE VERY FINE (VF-30) — Light even wear is visible on the surface, with wear being more evident on the highest points. All lettering and major features remain sharp.

VERY FINE (VF-20) — The design exhibits moderate wear on all high points. All major details are clear.

FINE (F-12) — A moderate to considerably worn coin, but still a collectible specimen. The basic outline must still be very clear. All lettering, including the word "LIBERTY" (on coins with this feature on the shield or headband) is visible, but with some weaknesses.

Fine   Very good

VERY GOOD (VG-8) — A much worn but not altogether unattractive coin. Coins in this condition should be free of major gouges or other mutilations, but they may be somewhat scratched from use.

GOOD (G-4) — A heavily worn coin. The major designs are visible but faint in many areas. The date and mint mark must be legible to qualify the coin for this rating.

ABOUT GOOD (AG-3) — A barely minimum-condition coin that is very heavily worn, with portions of the date, lettering, and legends worn smooth. The date may be barely readable.

POOR — Coins in poor condition are usually highly undesirable and considered uncollectible. They may be bent, corroded, or completely worn down.

As in the case of coins struck for circulation, proof coins can also be graded according to the Sheldon scale. Utilizing this numbering system, the American Numismatic Association places proofs into four major condition categories:

PERFECT PROOF (Proof-70) — A coin with no handling marks, hairlines, or other defects. There must not be a single flaw. The Proof-70 may be brilliant or have natural toning.

CHOICE PROOF (Proof-65) — This refers to a proof coin which may have a few very fine hairlines, generally from friction-type cleaning or drying after rubbing or dipping. To the unaided eye, it appears to be virtually perfect, but five-power magnification reveals some minute lines.

PROOF (Proof-60) — This designation refers to a proof with a number of handling marks and hairlines which are visible to the naked eye.

IMPAIRED PROOFS — If a proof has been excessively cleaned, has numerous marks, scratches, dents, or other flaws, it is categorized as an "impaired proof." If the coin shows extensive wear, then it is assigned one of the lesser grades: Proof-55, Proof-45, etc. It isn't logical to label a slightly worn proof as AU (about uncirculated) for it was never circulated to begin with — thus, the term "impaired proof" is appropriate.

UNC. (MS-60)

To accurately determine the condition of a specific coin, collectors usually examine it with a magnifying glass. This enlarged photo of an uncirculated Lincoln cent reveals sharp, clear details in the hair and beard. The grains of the wheat stalk stand out sharply on the reverse.

(EF-40)

The first traces of wear appear on the highest points of the obverse design, the cheek and jawbone. The inside row of grains also shows slight wear.

(VF-20)

Moderate signs of wear show around the ear and a smooth spot is evident at the top of the ear on coins in this condition. The grains of wheat near the top of the stalk are less distinct.

(F-12)

Considerable wear appears on coins in this condition. The back and bottom edges are less distinct and the cheek and jawbone are fairly worn. The parallel lines of the wheat stalk have smooth areas.

(VG-8)

All fine detail is gone from the hair and beard. Only a rough outline
of the ear is visible and the end of the bow tie is vague. Only portions
of the parallel lines of the wheat stalk remain.

(G-4)

On this very much worn coin the hairline is indistinct, the area
between the cheek and jaw is completely smooth and only a trace of
the ear remains. Only the vaguest outline of the grains can be seen.

ABOUT GOOD (AG-3)

Coins worn to this point show only the silhouette of the head. Even the outlines of the shirt and coat collar are worn smooth. The rims of the coin are quite flat.

POOR

These minimum condition coins are generally unattractive and may be pitted, corroded, dark or even bent. Coins that are so badly worn are not worth collecting except possibly as space fillers for rare dates.

Points of highest wear on U.S. coins

On each different coin design there are certain key points to inspect in order to assign a condition grade to any given specimen. The most important parts of a coin design, so far as the process of grading is concerned, are the points of highest wear. Every coin has certain features of the design that stand out from the remainder of the coin and these are the first areas to bump or rub against other coins or objects. The absence or presence of wear on these high points determine whether a coin is uncirculated or used. The relative amount of wear on a used coin determines its exact grade as shown on the preceding pages in the enlarged photographs of Lincoln cents over a range of conditions.

JEFFERSON NICKELS: *Wear first appears on Jefferson's eyebrow, cheekbone, and the lower back part of his hair. On the reverse, the first signs of wear show on the steps and on the outline of the lintel above the doorway of Monticello.*

ROOSEVELT DIMES: *The hair just above the ear is the first point to show wear. On the reverse, wear appears first on the lines of the flame.*

WASHINGTON QUARTERS: *The first traces of wear on this design appear on the hair just back of the ear. The first spots of wear on the reverse show on the eagle's breast and the tops of the legs.*

FRANKLIN HALF DOLLARS: *The hair above and back of the ear and the curl at the end of the strands show the first traces of wear. On the reverse, wear first shows on the highest part of the horizontal lines at the top of the bell and on the horizontal lines at the bottom just above the clapper.*

TYPE COLLECTING

The plan of a type collection is to let one coin represent many others. Usually this means that one of the commonest and thus least expensive dates or varieties is used to represent all the other coins, including expensive rarities that are of the same design style or "type." Nearly every collector of older

1938   1943

These four Egyptian coins, all of the same denomination, are different types. The two above are minor varieties, showing the same design on differently shaped planchets. The two coins below are major "face different" types.

1954   1960

The legends on the coins above are in Arabic and the dates are written in Arabic numerals, not the so-called "Arabic numerals" used in Western countries, but the true Arabic numerals upon which our own are based. Using the table below, can you make out the dates on the left edge of the reverses? The dates at the right edge are the equivalent Moslem A. H. dates (for conversion formula, see page 154).

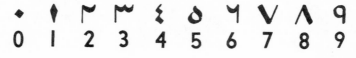

٠	١	٢	٣	٤	٥	٦	٧	٨	٩
0	1	2	3	4	5	6	7	8	9

Collectors regard the two designs of the 1883 Liberty Head nickel as different "types." The variety without "CENTS" was issued first, but unscrupulous people gold-plated them and passed them off as $5 gold pieces. To remedy the situation, the word "CENTS" was added to the later issues and continued to appear on subsequent dates.

coins soon abandons series collecting—having a specimen of every date and variety—and instead collects a single coin of each type.

Collectors are seldom in agreement as to just how much or how little alteration of the design creates a different type. If your interests are wide, if you collect coins of all the world or a fair portion of it, you will probably be concerned only with major, obviously different types. On the other hand, if you limit your activity to the coins of just one country, you will surely want some of the minor types and varieties to fill out your collection. The U.S. type coins illustrated show only the major "face different" varieties and demonstrate how a type collection of the silver and minor metal issues can be planned and organized.

There were two styles of 1839 Seated Liberty half dollars, with and without a fold of drapery at the elbow. This is considered a minor variation, not really a great enough difference to create separate "types."

43

Major design types of U.S. coins

1a   2

1b

HALF CENTS

1. *1793–1797, Liberty Head with Cap on Pole
— a. 1793 only, head left; b. 1794–1797, head
right.* 2. *1800–1808, Draped Bust of Liberty.*
3. *1809–1835, Turban Head of Liberty.* 4.
1849–1857, Liberty Head with Coronet.

3   4

LARGE CENTS

5a   6

5b

5. *1793 only, Liberty Head with Flowing
Hair — a. 1793 only, chain reverse; b.
1793 only, wreath reverse.* 6. *1793–
1796, Liberty Head with Cap on Pole.*
7. *1796–1807, Draped Bust of Liberty.*
8. *1808–1814, Turban Head of Liberty.*
9. *1816–1857, Liberty Head with Coronet.*

7   8   9

10   11a   11b

12a

12b

SMALL CENTS

10. *1857–1858, Flying Eagle.* 11. *1859–1909, Indian Head* – a. *1859 only, olive wreath, no shield;* b. *1860–1909, oak wreath, with shield.* 12. *1909–   , Lincoln Head* – a. *1909–1958, wheat spray reverse;* b. *1959–   , Lincoln Memorial reverse.*

TWO CENTS

13. *1864–1873, Shield.*

13

THREE CENTS (SILVER)

14. *1851–1873, Shield on star.*

15

14

THREE CENTS (NICKEL)

15. *1865–1889, Liberty Head.*

16　　　　　　17a　　　　　17b

HALF DIMES (SILVER FIVE CENTS)

18

16. *1794–1795, Liberty Head with Flowing Hair.* 17. *1796–1805, Draped Bust of Liberty — a. 1796–1797, standing eagle reverse; b. 1800–1805, heraldic eagle reverse.* 18. *1829–1837, Liberty Head Wearing Cap.* 19. *1837–1873, Seated Figure of Liberty.*

19

FIVE CENTS (NICKEL)

20　　　　　　21　　　　　22　　　　　23

20. *1866–1883, Shield.* 21. *1883–1912, Liberty Head with Coronet.* 22. *1913–1938, Indian Head, Buffalo reverse.* 23. *1938– Jefferson Head.*

DIMES

24a

24b

25

24. *1796–1807, Draped Bust of Liberty
— a. 1796–1797, standing eagle reverse;
b. 1798–1807, heraldic eagle reverse.*
25. *1809–1837, Liberty Head Wearing
Cap.* 26. *1837–1891, Seated Figure of
Liberty.* 27. *1892–1916, Liberty Head
with Cap and Wreath.* 28. *1916–1945,
Liberty Head with Winged Cap.* 29.
1946–　, Roosevelt Head.

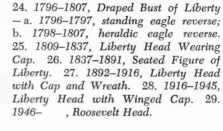

26

27

28

29

30

TWENTY CENTS

30. *1875–1878, Seated Figure
of Liberty.*

**QUARTER
DOLLARS**

31. *1796–1807, Draped Bust of Liberty – a.
1796 only, standing eagle reverse; b. 1804–
1807, heraldic eagle reverse.*

31a

31b

QUARTER DOLLARS

32. *1815–1838, Liberty Head Wearing Cap.*
33. *1838–1891, Seated Figure of Liberty.* 34.
1892–1916, Liberty Head with Cap and Wreath.
35. *1916–1930, Standing Figure of Liberty.*
36. *1932–   , Washington Head.* 36a. *dated*
1976, Bicentennial.

HALF DOLLARS

HALF DOLLARS

38b

37. *1794-1795, Liberty Head with Flowing Hair.* 38. *1796–1807, Draped Bust of Liberty* – a. *1796–1797, standing eagle reverse;* b. *1801–1807, heraldic eagle reverse.* 39. *1807–1839, Liberty Head Wearing Cap.* 40. *1839–1891, Seated Figure of Liberty.* 41. *1892–1915, Liberty Head with Cap and Wreath.* 42. *1916–1947, Walking Figure of Liberty.* 43. *1948–1963, Franklin Head.* 44. *1964– , Kennedy Head. See next page.* 44a. *dated 1976, Bicentennial.*

39

40

42

41

43

45. *1794–1795, Liberty Head with Flowing Hair.* 46. *1795–1804, Draped Bust of Liberty – a. 1795–1798, standing eagle reverse; b. 1798–1804, heraldic eagle reverse.* 47. *1840–1873, Seated Figure of Liberty.* 48. *1878–1921, Liberty Head with Cap and Wreath.* 49. *1921–1935, Radiant Head of Liberty.* 50. *1971– , Eisenhower Head.* 50a. *dated 1979, Susan B. Anthony.*

44   44a   45   46a   46b

50

47

48

49

50

51

SILVER DOLLARS

50a. The copper-nickel clad Susan B. Anthony dollar, first issued in 1979, is slightly larger than a quarter. Because it can be so easily confused with the quarter, the Anthony dollar did not circulate well and was discontinued after 1981.

TRADE DOLLARS

51. *1873–1885, Seated Figure of Liberty.*

51

U.S. GOLD COINS

American gold coins were issued fairly regularly from 1795 until the gold standard was abandoned in 1933. Today, some Americans have never seen a gold coin and for others they are just fond memories. Of the many millions of dollars' worth of gold coins struck over the years, a comparative handful repose in coin collections and are among their owners' most prized possessions. Every serious collection should contain at least one gold coin as a representative of the important role gold has played in coinage history.

Dollars were the lowest denomination gold coin issued by the U.S. government. Three different styles were used between 1849 and 1889.

The $3 gold piece, introduced in 1854, paralleled a reduction of the letter rate to 3¢ and was intended to facilitate postal transactions.

Gold coins were regularly issued in six denominations comprising eleven principal types, excluding the early dates. The types are: small (1849–54) and large (1854–89) gold dollars; Liberty (1840–1907) and Indian Head (1908–29) quarter eagles ($2.50); three dollars (1854–89); Liberty (1839–1908) and Indian Head (1908–29) half eagles ($5); Liberty (1838–1907) and Indian Head (1907–33) eagles ($10); and Liberty Head (1850–1907) and Standing Liberty (1907–32) double eagles ($20).

The eagle ($10) was the first gold denomination struck and the quarter, half and double eagle pieces are based on this unit.

New collectors often wonder why the $20 coin, the largest denomination regularly issued, was not called the eagle and the other pieces fractions thereof. The answer is simple: the first gold coins struck were the $5 and $10 pieces of 1795. The unit designation of "eagle" was given to the larger coin, the $10. The $20 piece was not introduced until 55 years later in 1850 and by that time the $10 eagle was firmly established.

The usual first project of collectors of U.S. gold coins is to assemble a type set of eleven coins representing the major

The double eagle ($20) is the highest denomination regularly issued
U.S. gold coin.

issues. All gold coins are fairly expensive and most collectors
build their sets one piece at a time. The next most popular
assortment is a six-piece set, one coin of each denomination
from $1 to $20. By limiting the set to the eagle values only
($2½, 5, 10, 20) the cost can be brought down still more. Even
if your budget allows for only one gold coin, this single piece
will enhance the attractiveness of your collection and greatly
increase the pleasure you get from showing your coins.

The Indian Head $2½ and $5 gold pieces do not have raised borders
as do most other coins; the design and lettering are incuse in the
planchet. President Theodore Roosevelt objected to using the Deity's
name on coins, and some of the $10 and $20 pieces of 1907 and 1908
are without the "In God We Trust." Congress restored it in 1908, for
all succeeding issues.

The high relief, Roman numeral double eagle of 1907 is usually regarded as the most beautiful coin ever produced at a U.S. mint. It was designed by the noted sculptor, Augustus Saint-Gaudens.

Displaying type coins

Specially designed albums are available for the type coin collections of several different countries. Non-collectors particularly enjoy looking at type collections because every coin is different and has a separate story to go with it. By collecting types you can own and learn about many older, historically interesting coins, yet keep the cost at a level that is not prohibitive.

This album contains a space for each major "type" of U.S. coin issued from 1793 to the present. Since each coin in such a collection is different in design, this makes an attractive and interesting display.

THREE CENT (Silver)
1851

Single outline star
as issued 1851-1854

Type #22

(Left) 2″ × 2″ individual holders are ideal for displaying collections of assorted coins. They are available with different size openings. (Right) 2″ × 2″ coin envelopes provide space for a complete write-up about the coin. Many enveloped coins can be stored in a small space.

A similar plan can be used to collect the coins of any nation by type. The independent coinages of many countries are fairly recent, but others date back for centuries. The cost or scarcity of the early coins may force you to choose an arbitrary starting point for your collection. Usually you can find a logical starting point in a nation's coinage history. For the European nations, the Napoleonic period draws a line between what might be called "old" and "modern" coins.

The type-collection approach can be applied to rulers as well as design types. You can use one coin to represent all the coins issued by the same ruler. This sort of collection is especially pleasing to those who are interested in the political history of a country. Early English coins are frequently collected this way. A set of English shillings is shown of one of each of the British monarchs back to Henry VIII, who first regularly issued the denomination. Coins of diverse denominations could just as well have been used to add variety, but some collectors prefer to show coins more nearly uniform in size, which demonstrates again how well coin collecting can suit the individual.

56

Type collection of English monarchs shown on their shillings

Edward VI

Henry VIII

Elizabeth I

Philip
and Mary

James I

Charles I

Charles II

Commonwealth

William
and Mary

James II

William III

Anne

George I

George II

George III

George IV

William IV

Victoria

Edward VII

George V

George VI

Elizabeth II

COINS FROM MANY COUNTRIES

The first advice the new collector is likely to get is that he cannot collect everything and therefore must specialize. Since over the centuries, thousands upon thousands of coins have been struck, it is obviously true that no one can hope to have a specimen of every issue. It doesn't necessarily follow, however, that you must restrict your interest to coins of just one country, one size, one era, or one topic. Every coin you come across has a story to tell, whether it is from a great nation or tiny island. If you want to put together a collection of coins that appeals to you for no other reason than that you find them interesting, go ahead and do so. Don't be afraid to collect coins just for the fun of it.

Collecting coins from as many different coin-issuing states as possible is extremely interesting and will teach you a great

Afghanistan,
1961 5 Afghani

Zambia, 1964
2 shillings

About one hundred and fifty different nations and colonies, ranging from Afghanistan to Zambia, are now issuing coins. An interesting way to begin a collection is to get a single coin from as many different countries as possible.

deal about geography. You will come to know the identifying features of each nation's coinage, develop a familiarity with words in various languages, and pick up quite a bit of history. About one hundred and fifty nations and colonies issue coins at the present time, but hundreds of other cities, principalities, duchies, former kingdoms, and former colonies have had their own coinage in times gone by.

Latvia, Lithuania, and Estonia disappeared as coin-issuing nations at the start of World War II. Serbia and Montenegro disappeared in World War I. The Kingdom of the Two Sicilies ceased issuing coins upon the unification of Italy in 1861. There are hundreds of similar examples back over the centuries; yet coins of these places still exist, many in sufficient quantity to turn up frequently in collections and dealers' stocks.

Lithuania, 1925 50 centu   *Serbia, 1875 2 dinars*

Including obsolete coinages in a collection greatly increases the number of different nations that can be represented.

Coin-Issuing Nations of the World

Afars and Issas	Bahrain
Afghanistan	Bangladesh
Albania	Barbados
Algeria	Belgium
Angola	Belize
Argentina	Bermuda
Australia	Bhutan
Austria	Bolivia
Bahamas	Brazil

British Virgin Islands
Brunei
Bulgaria
Burma
Burundi
Cambodia
Cameroon
Canada
Cape Verde Islands
Cayman Islands
Central African Republic
Chile
China, People's Republic
Cocos (Keeling) Islands
Colombia
Comoro Islands
Cook Islands
Costa Rica
Cuba
Cyprus
Czechoslovakia
Denmark
Djibouti
Dominican Republic
Ecuador
Egypt
Equatorial African States
Equatorial Guinea
Ethiopia
Fiji
Finland
France
French Polynesia
Gabon
Gambia
Germany—East & West
Ghana
Gibraltar

Great Britain
Greece
Guatemala
Guernsey
Guinea
Guyana
Haiti
Honduras
Hong Kong
Hungary
Iceland
India
Indonesia
Iran
Iraq
Ireland
Isle of Man
Israel
Italy
Jamaica
Japan
Jersey
Jordan
Kenya
Korea—North & South
Kuwait
Laos
Lebanon
Lesotho
Liberia
Libya
Luxembourg
Macau
Malagasy Republic
Malawi
Malaysia
Maldive Islands
Mali

Malta
Mauritania
Mauritius
Mexico
Monaco
Mongolia
Morocco
Mozambique
Nepal
Netherlands
Netherlands Antilles
New Caledonia
New Hebrides
New Zealand
Nicaragua
Nigeria
Norway
Oman
Pakistan
Panama
Paraguay
Peru
Philippines
Poland
Portugal
Portuguese Guinea
Qatar and Dubai
Reunion
Rumania
Russia
Rwanda
St. Helena
St. Thomas & Prince Islands
Salvador
San Marino
Saudi Arabia
Seychelles

Sierra Leone
Singapore
Somalia
South Africa
Southern Yemen
Spain
Sri Lanka
Sudan
Surinam
Sweden
Switzerland
Syria
Taiwan
Tanzania
Tchad
Thailand
Tibet
Timor
Togo
Tonga
Trinidad & Tobago
Tunisia
Turkey
Turks and Caicos Islands
Uganda
United Arab Emirates
United States
Uruguay
Vatican City
Venezuela
Viet Nam
West African States
Western Samoa
Yemen
Yugoslavia
Zaire
Zambia
Zimbabwe

PROOF COIN SETS

These are special products of a mint made for coin collectors or for official presentations. They are generally available as full sets often attractively boxed or packaged. Proof coins might be described more meaningfully as "specimen" or "display" sets. The metal blanks for proof coins are carefully selected and cleaned. They are struck from dies which are kept clean and polished. The result is a coin with a brilliant mirror-like surface, sharp edges and perfect detail. At all stages, the coins are carefully handled and never allowed to come into contact with one another.

In the U.S., proof coins were struck in small numbers during the earliest years of coinage and on a more or less regular basis from 1858 through 1915. Proof coinage resumed in 1936 and except for lapses in 1943–49 and 1965–67 has continued on an annual basis. Prior to 1968, all proofs were made at the Philadelphia mint. Beginning with that date, however, production was switched to San Francisco.

Proof sets can be ordered at certain times each year directly from the San Francisco Assay Office. For price information and ordering instructions, write to 155 Hermann St., San Francisco, CA 94102.

Current sets and proof sets of earlier years can, of course, be purchased at a premium from dealers or collectors who had the foresight to put away a few extra sets.

Philadelphia mint proof sets issued during the late 1950's and early 1960's were sealed in a special cellophane wrapper within a brown paper envelope.

Current U.S. proof sets, struck at the San Francisco Assay Office, are packaged in solid plastic, imprinted holders.

Proof coins are produced in many of the world's mints and are frequently housed in handsome presentation cases. The number of sets produced in any given year is usually quite limited.

The 1972 Bahamas proof set, typical of many recent issues, was supplied in a satin- and velvet-lined presentation case.

Specialized Collecting

Eventually, almost every collector finds that one phase of collecting has a particular appeal so he decides to concentrate his attention on that area. He may, of course, pursue a specialty in conjunction with the more usual date and mint mark collections. Through years of interest in numismatics, it is not unusual for a collector to concentrate at different times on various phases of the hobby.

COINS OF A GROUP OF COUNTRIES

British, French or Portuguese colonial coins are often collected as a unit. Other popularly collected groups of coins are those of Scandinavia, Africa, Latin America, Germany, the Benelux Countries, Spain and Portugal, and the Orient. Many of the new nations of Africa are just beginning to issue their own coins and these are sure to grow in interest.

*Jamaica, 1964
penny*

*Tanzania, 1966
1 shilling*

FAO coins

A brand new possibility for collecting opened up in 1968 with the start of the first international coin issue. Launched under the auspices of the Food and Agriculture Organization of the United Nations, the FAO coin plan is intended to draw attention to one of the great problems of our times—that of providing food for the expanding world population. Where they are used in circulation, these special coins serve as daily reminders of the problem. Their purchase by collectors provides funds for agricultural development. The "profit" on the coins comes from the difference between the intrinsic metal value and their higher face value (called seigniorage). The coins themselves carry messages such as "Grow More Food."

Nearly 100 nations have authorized coins under the FAO coin plan and several billion pieces have already been released. All of the coins are legal tender in the country of issue and many are low denomination coins released into normal circulation. A few issues, however, were produced in small numbers primarily for collectors. Individual FAO coins are available from dealers and various agencies. The FAO organization has also assembled special albums which are sold by the page as the coins are released.

Uganda, 1968 5 shillings. National arms with ankole cow and calf. One of the first FAO issues, this coin publicizes the drive in Uganda to increase livestock production. The Bank of Uganda made 100,000 pieces available for general use and an additional 5,000 proof specimens were prepared for collectors.

*Bahrain, 1969
250 fils,* FIAT
PANIS — Latin for
"Let There Be Bread"

Bolivia, 1968 1 peso,
GUERRA CONTRA EL
HAMBRE—Spanish for
"War Against Hunger"

*Ceylon, 1968 2
rupees,* "GROW MORE
FOOD" in English,
Sinhala and Tamil

Rwanda, 1970 2 francs,
AUGMENTONS LA
PRODUCTION—French for
"Let Us Increase Production"

Iran, 1969 10 rials,
"Who Sows Wheat Sows
Truth" in Persian

68

India, 1970 10 rupees. The lotus floating on water is a symbol of prosperity. The reverse shows the Asoka Pillar, emblem of India. This coin was released on October 16, 1970, the Food and Agriculture Organization's 25th anniversary.

Singapore, 1971 5 cents. A total mintage of ten million pieces is scheduled for this low denomination coin which will be used along with similar issues of other nations in a world-wide promotion of the FAO food goals.

Iraq, 1970 25 fils. The date palms are symbolic of the fact that Iraq produces 80 per cent of the world's date exports. The edge has the letters FAO in relief.

FAO COIN ALBUM

BAHRAIN

DOMINICAN REPUBLIC

ZAMBIA

GUYANA

JORDAN

CHINA

TRINIDAD AND TOBAGO

IRAN

MONEDAS INSPIRADAS POR LA FAO

TOPICAL COLLECTING

Coin collectors can borrow a technique that is very popular among stamp collectors—"topical" or thematic collecting. In a topical collection, the coins are related to one another on the basis of their design and the people or objects shown. Coins do not present quite the diversity of design found on stamps, but several subjects, such as animals and birds, are especially well represented. The range of the animal kingdom, from elephants to bees, can be found on coins. The 5-franc piece from the African nation of Mali gave us the first hippopotamus on a coin in 1961.

Mali, 1961 5 francs

Topical collections can also be based on the themes expressed by coins. Religion is a popular topic among stamp collectors and many coins fit this category too, showing churches, popes, saints, and mottoes with a religious tone, such as "In God We Trust" on U.S. coins.

Looking through a coin catalogue will suggest various subjects for a topical collection. By combing the listings and illustrations in a world-wide catalogue, and by watching the new issues of the world for appropriate designs, you will add to your collection and keep your enthusiasm high.

(Opposite) Page 3 of the FAO coin album. The release price has averaged about $20.00 per page and the album issue has been limited to 7,000–10,000 world-wide.

Animals on coins

Bull

Antelope

Llama

Giraffes

Beaver

Polar bear

Elephant

Crocodile

Dog

Kangaroo

Tiger

Lion

Jaguar

Turtle

Moose

72

Sailing ship

Native craft

The *Matthew*

Sailing ship

The *Mayflower*

Viking ship

Sloop
and dinghy

Caravel

The *Golden Hind*

Galley

Dhow

School ship

Sailing ship

Clipper ship

Dhow and
modern steamer

Galley

77

Religious themes on coins

Pope Paul VI

Menorah

Martin Luther

Buddhist prayer
wheel and temple
bell

Ecumenical
Council

Indian
totem pole

Chanukah lamp

Christ and
apostles
in boat

Madonna and child

Maori tiki

78

St. Charles Church,
Vienna, Austria

Ark of the Torah

Moslem Mosque

St. Cyril and
St. Methodius

Nativity
scene

St.
Wenceslaus

Daniel in the
lions' den

St. Marinus

St. George

St. Stephen

St. John
the Baptist

Unusual shape coins

Coins struck on unusually shaped planchets make an interesting collection. The different shapes enable people to recognize coins of various denominations without looking at them closely. The central-hole coins are sometimes strung together by natives, but they also serve the purpose of allowing for larger planchets using the same amount of metal as a smaller, non-hole coin.

COMMEMORATIVE COLLECTING

Many commemoratives have been issued as crown-size coins, but other sizes have been used just as frequently. Commemoratives have designs and legends that mark important occasions, recall historic events, or glorify famous men. A few examples of modern coins issued to record events at the time

Austria, 1955 25 shillings, figure with lyre and Greek mask (reopening of the Vienna Opera House)

Belgium, 1958 50 francs, head of King Baudouin and the City Hall on Brussels Grand Place (Brussels World's Fair)

they happened are those struck for the reopening of the Vienna Opera House in 1955, the World Fairs — in Belgium in 1958 and Japan in 1970 — and the Olympic Games — in Finland in 1952, Japan in 1964, Mexico in 1968, Germany in 1972, Canada in 1976, the U.S.S.R. in 1980, and the United States in 1984. South Korea plans a coin set to commemorate the 1988 games in Seoul.

Sometimes more than one country commemorates the same event, as with the 1964 Danish and Greek coins for the wedding

Finland,
1952 500 markkaa
(15th Olympic Games)

Japan,
1964 1,000 yen
(18th Olympic Games)

Mexico,
1968 25 pesos
(19th Olympic
Games)

Germany,
10 marks dated 1972
(20th Olympic Games)

Canada,
10 dollars dated 1976
(21st Olympic Games)

Denmark, 1964 5 Kroner
(wedding commemorative)

Greece, 1963 30 drachmai
(wedding commemorative)

of Princess Anne-Marie and King Constantine. Other coins that are now old, such as the 1871 taler of Saxony marking the victorious conclusion of the Franco-Prussian War, were, nevertheless, struck at the time of the event they celebrate. When viewed in collections today, these older coins recall the events of years gone by that were important to the people of their time.

Saxony, 1871 taler, Johann I. Victory on horseback (conclusion of Franco-Prussian War)

*Italy, 1961 500 lire (100th anniversary of the
unification of the Italian states)*

*Ceylon, 1957 rupee (commemorates the 2500th
anniversary of the death of Buddha)*

Most modern commemoratives recall events of times past;
they are frequently issued to celebrate the anniversary of some
military or political achievement. The centennial (one-
hundredth anniversary) of an event is perhaps most often
celebrated with a coin as, for example, the 1961 Italian 500-lire
piece struck to commemorate the 1861 unification of the
individual Italian states into the nation of Italy as we know it
today. Events commemorated on recent coins are as far
distant in time as 544 B.C., recalled on the 1957 coins of
Ceylon struck on the 2500th anniversary of Buddha's attain-
ment of Nirvana.

Finally, commemoratives pay respect to famous men and
mark events in the lives of people as well as of nations. Birth
years, death years, weddings, wedding anniversaries, anniversaries of the reign—all have been celebrated with coins.
Great Britain issued a special crown in 1953 for the coronation

of Queen Elizabeth II and another in 1965 in memorializing Winston Churchill. A Danish 5-kroner piece of 1960 commemorates the silver wedding anniversary of King Frederick and Queen Ingrid. Besides statesmen and rulers, coins have recognized discoverers and explorers, builders, physicians and scientists, writers and musicians, religious leaders and saints.

Prussia, 1861 taler, Wilhelm I (coronation issue)

Sweden, 1897 2 kronor, Oscar II (25th year of reign)

Greece, 1963 30 drachmai, Paul I (100th year of the dynasty)

Countries with monarchs often strike commemorative coins to celebrate coronations, anniversaries of the reign, and occasionally to memorialize a whole dynasty.

Denmark, 1958 2 kroner, Frederick IX (18th birthday of Princess Margrethe)

Belgium, 1960 50 francs, Baudouin I (marriage to Queen Fabiola)

Private events of monarchs' lives, such as birthdays and weddings, are also recorded on special commemorative coins.

Philippines, 1947 peso (commemorating General MacArthur)

Commemoratives are by no means limited to royalty, but it is unusual for a commoner, no matter how deserving, to be memorialized during his lifetime. It has happened, however, as with General Douglas MacArthur on coins of the Philippines.

Italy, 1965 500 lire (700th anniversary of the birth of the poet Dante)

Commemoratives more often are memorial coins issued after the death of a great man, like the Churchill crown. Sometimes, recognition comes centuries later, as on the coin above.

Russia, 1970 ruble (100th anniversary of the birth of Lenin)

Most commemorative coins of famous men are issued to celebrate an anniversary of their birth. Some countries, however, mark the anniversary of their death.

Luxembourg, 1946 50 francs (600th anniversary of death of John the Blind)

The pair of German coins below are unusual in that they mark both the birth year and death day, "Todestag," of the poet Friedrich von Schiller.

Germany, 1934
5 marks (175th
anniversary of birth
of Schiller)

German, 1955 5 marks (150th anniversary
of death of Schiller

Finland, 1970 10 markkaa (100th anniversary of birth of statesman Juho
Kusti Paasikivi)

Commemorative coins are issued to celebrate events as well as people. Here are examples of coins issued contemporaneously with the event, on a centennial anniversary and, amazingly, on a 1000th anniversary.

Ceylon, 1957 5 rupees (2,500 years of Buddhism)

Germany, 1929 3 marks (1000th anniversary of Meissen)

Peru, 1965 20 soles (400th anniversary of Lima mint)

Portugal, 1966 20 escudos (opening of Salazar Bridge at Lisbon)

89

In September 1985 the Mexico City Mint released its first five proof coins in its long history, commemorating the World Cup of Soccer staged at Mexico City in the summer of 1986.

The two highest denominations — 500 and 250 pesos — are struck in gold, while the three lower denominations — 100, 50, and 25 pesos — are struck in silver. The common obverse is Mexico's national coat of arms (F), with the reverses depicting the following: (A) 500 pesos — a soccer ball superimposed over the famed silver coin, the "piece of eight," with the legend *450 años de la casa de moneda* marking the 450th anniversary of the Mexico City Mint, which was established on May 11, 1535 by the royal decree of Spain's Charles I. (B) 250 pesos — Liberty on horseback, with a soccer ball in the background. (C) 100 pesos — a modern defensive soccer player heading the ball away from the net. (D) 50 pesos — a pre-Columbian athlete playing a form of soccer called *Pot a Pok*. (E) 25 pesos — two pre-Columbian architectural designs above a modern soccer ball. All coins are inscribed with "M̊," the Mexico City Mint mark.

At the time of the completion of the World Cup of Soccer in 1986, the Mexico City Mint produced 11 additional commemorative coins, two in gold and nine in silver.

A. *500 pesos*   B. *250 pesos*   C. *100 pesos*

Mexico's first proof coins commemorate the 1986 World Cup Soccer games.

D. *50 pesos*   E. *25 pesos*   F. *Mexico's coat of arms,
                                                  the common obverse*

U.S. commemoratives

The first U.S. commemorative, a half dollar for the Columbian Exposition, shows Christopher Columbus and his ship, the *Santa Maria*.

Of the 50 different types of U.S. silver commemoratives issued up to 1954, all are half dollars except the 1893 Isabella quarter and the 1900 Lafayette dollar. Several of the halves were struck during more than one year and/or at more than one mint. Counting all of the date and mint mark varieties, there are 144 coins in the series issued between 1892 and 1954. U.S. coin catalogs always include illustrations, mintage figures and data on each coin.

The Isabella quarter is the only commemorative of this denomination as well as the only U.S. coin displaying the portrait of a foreign monarch.

A number of the U.S. commemoratives are rare, only 10,008 pieces having been issued of the Hawaiian Sesquicentennial, the Hudson Sesquicentennial and the Old Spanish Trail coins. Many of the individual date and mint mark varieties were issued in even smaller quantity, the lowest coinage being the 1938 Daniel Boone coins. Only 2,100 pieces of this date were struck at each of the three mints. This means that 10,008 is the

The Hawaiian Sesquicentennial half dollar is one of the rarest commemorative types. The total coinage was 10,008 pieces.

U.S., 1922 half dollar (centennial of birth of Ulysses S. Grant)

 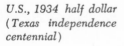

U.S., 1934 half dollar (Texas independence centennial)

U.S., 1925 half dollar (battles of Lexington and Concord)

U.S., 1936 half dollar
(San Francisco-
Oakland Bay Bridge)

U.S. 1926 half dollar
(Oregon Trail Memorial)

The Lafayette dollar of 1900 was the first silver commemorative of this
denomination and the first U.S. coin to have a portrait of an American
president. The statue on the reverse represents a memorial erected in
Paris as a gift of the American people.

maximum number of type sets that can ever be completed and
2,100 the maximum number of full sets of all varieties.

The cost of completing even a type set today amounts to
hundreds of dollars. Many of the commemoratives, however,
were issued in large enough numbers to be within the reach of
the average collector. Even though you may not aspire to the
whole set, you will find that a few commemoratives add interest

to any kind of collection. The Columbian Pilgrim, Monroe Doctrine, Lexington-Concord, Stone Mountain, Sesquicentennial of American Independence, Oregon Trail and Daniel Boone coins are all of national interest and still available in uncirculated condition for fairly modest prices. You may find too, that one of the commemoratives was issued for your own state or locality and would surely be appropriate for your collection.

This U.S. commemorative half dollar, issued in 1951–54, shows two famous Black Americans, Booker T. Washington and George Washington Carver.

After 1954 the U.S. Mint suspended the production of commemorative coins for more than 20 years. Mint and Treasury officials felt that striking coins for circulation purposes took precedence over all other matters.

Then in 1975–76 the U.S. produced a quasi-commemorative coinage when the regular-issue quarters, half dollars, and dollars were inscribed with special reverses to mark the American Bicentennial. These three denominations featured the following designs: (a) Washington quarter with colonial drummer, (b) Kennedy half dollar with Independence Hall in Philadelphia, (c) Eisenhower dollar with the Liberty Bell superimposed upon the moon. The obverses of all three coins remained unchanged except for the dual dating "1776–1976." They were all struck during 1975 and 1976 for general circulation as well as being included in proof and uncirculated sets. Most numismatic writers and historians don't consider these American Bicentennial coins to be true commemoratives since they were issued for general circulation.

The first authentic U.S. commemorative to come out in 28

years was the 1982 silver half dollar marking the 250th anniversary of the birth of George Washington. This was also the first 90 percent silver coin produced by the U.S. Mint since 1964. Designed by Elizabeth Jones, chief sculptor and engraver at the U.S. Mint, the coin's obverse portrays George Washington astride a horse, while the reverse depicts the eastern façade of Mount Vernon, Washington's Virginia mansion on the Potomac, some 15 miles south of Washington, D.C. The coin was struck in both uncirculated and proof versions with both being sold at premiums.

In 1983–84 the U.S. Mint came forth with a series of three coins to commemorate the 23rd International Olympic Summer Games in Los Angeles. There are two $1 silver coins, one dated 1983 and the other 1984. The 1983 dollar features on the obverse side a representation of Myron's ancient classic sculpture "The Discus Thrower," while the reverse depicts the head and upper body of the American eagle. The 1984 dollar has on the obverse side Robert Graham's sculpture facing the Los Angeles Memorial Coliseum, with the reverse side showing the full American eagle.

The Los Angeles Olympic Games series was magnificently completed with a 1984 $10 gold eagle, the first U.S. gold piece issued in over 50 years, and the first U.S. gold commemorative to appear since 1926. The eagle's obverse side depicts two runners bearing the Olympic torch aloft, while the traditional eagle on the reverse side is modelled after the Great Seal of the United States. All three Olympic coins were sold at premiums with net proceeds donated to the Los Angeles Olympic Organizing Committee.

The U.S. Mint in 1986 released a series of three coins to commemorate the centennial of the Statue of Liberty: (1) a copper-nickel half dollar, (2) a silver dollar, (3) a $5 gold piece.

The designs on the obverse and reverse sides on the three coins are as follows: Half dollar — a large setting sun behind the New York skyline *circa* 1913, with the Statue of Liberty wel-

1986 Statue of Liberty Centennial Coins: (above) silver dollar, (left) half dollar, (below) $5 gold piece.

coming an ocean liner to transport immigrants on Ellis Island waiting to go to New York. Silver Dollar—the Statue of Liberty in front of the Ellis Island immigration facility with Liberty's hand holding her torch aloft, splitting the famous phrase from Emma Lazarus's poem, "The New Colossus." $5 gold piece—the head of the Statue of Liberty viewed from below, symbolizing the statue's gaze towards a future of freedom and opportunity, with a contemporary "landing" eagle paying homage to U.S. 19th-century gold coinage.

The U.S. Treasury levied surcharges on the three coins ($2 on each half dollar, $7 on each silver dollar, and $35 on each $5 gold piece, with those funds going towards the restoration and renovation of the Statue of Liberty and Ellis Island, and also for the establishment of an endowment to assure the continued upkeep and maintenance of these historic monuments.

(Left) Panama-Pacific commemorative gold dollar. (Center) Louisiana Purchase commemorative gold dollar. (Right) McKinley Memorial gold dollar. Only 15 different U.S. gold commemoratives have been issued.

There are also 15 gold commemorative coins: nine $1 pieces, two quarter eagles, one half eagle, one eagle, and the round and octagonal $50 gold pieces. Those 13 pieces issued up to 1926 are particularly rare, which puts them in great demand.

(Left) Panama-Pacific commemorative quarter eagle ($2½). (Right) 1926 Sesquicentennial of American Independence quarter eagle.

The commemoratives, of known and limited issue, have increased steadily in value over the years and have been perennial favorites with investment-minded collectors. Commemoratives were not intended for general use and are nearly always collected in uncirculated condition.

1915 Panama-Pacific $50 gold piece (quintuple eagle) with head of the Goddess Minerva in a crested helmet on the obverse, an owl—symbol of wisdom—perched on a pine branch on the reverse. Altogether, 645 pieces of the octagonal variety were issued, 483 pieces of the round.

CROWN OR TALER COLLECTING

Collectors use the word "crown" to describe coins approximating the size of the U.S. and Canadian dollars and the British five-shilling piece. While it is true that many crowned heads are shown on these large coins, the name actually derives from the fact that the first English silver coins of this size, dated 1551, were struck from fine silver (90% or more of the precious metal) called "crown" silver. The coin itself was equal in value to five shillings and was called a crown.

By the middle of the fifteenth century, European commerce had expanded to the point where there was a definite need for a large silver coin. The first dated issues of these new, large-size crowns were struck in 1486 by Archduke Sigismund at a mint in the Tyrol. Dollar-size coins were struck in quantity after the discovery in 1516 of a rich silver vein at Joachimsthal (Joachim's Valley) in the county of Schlick of the Kingdom of Bohemia. These large coins were called Joachimsthalers after their place of origin, but the coin's name was soon shortened

Bohemia, undated Joachimsthaler, Louis I (1516–26). Rampant double-tailed lion, LVDOVICVS PRIM D GRACIA R BO (Louis I, by the grace of God, King of Bohemia). Standing figure of St. Joachim (father of the Virgin Mary), AR DOMI SLI STE ET FRA CO D B (arms of the lords of Schlick, Stephen and his brothers, Counts of Bassano).

to "thaler," then as coins spread across the continent, changed to "taler" to "daalder" to "daler" to "dollar."

Crown collecting has become a very popular branch of numismatics. The large size of crowns allows for more detail on the coins and affords the designer space for artistic arrangement. These attractive coins are often rich in historical significance. Many of the recently issued pieces commemorate some specific event. Besides their beauty and historical connections, one of the attractions of coins is that you can handle them and enjoy their solid feel, and this is especially true of crowns. These large coins wear well and can usually be obtained in the better conditions. Large quantities of many issues were struck and these can be purchased at moderate prices.

More than 100 different states or nations have issued crown-size coins just since 1900. Many more countries and even cities issued crowns before the turn of the century, but most of the older issues are scarcer and more expensive than the later coins.

England, 1551 crown, Edward VI (1547–53). King in mail on horseback, EDVVARD VI DG AGL FRA Z HIBER REX (by the Grace of God, King of England, France and Ireland) *Quartered arms,* POSVI DEVM ADIVTORE MEVM *(I have made God my helper).* English monarchs included fleurs-de-lis in their coats of arms and claimed the throne of France in their titles until the nineteenth century.

Many collectors entering the crown field assemble collections representing as many different states as possible.

Special albums are on the market to accommodate this kind of collection. If you collect in this manner, you may want to stretch your budget as far as possible and select the least expensive issue of a country as an automatic choice without considering the others. You should, however, at least find out about all the available issues because you will sometimes find that a considerably more interesting or significant coin can be obtained for just a little extra expense.

You can also specialize in the crowns of one country or area. There have been more crowns from Germany than from any other nation. Many of the quite early coins can still be purchased for less than the cost of some of the modern coins issued within the past ten years.

Saxony, 1589 taler, Christian I (1586–91). Bust of Duke with sword, CHRISTIAN DG DVX SAXO SA ROMA IMP *(by the Grace of God, Duke of Saxony, of the Holy Roman Empire.) Multiple arms,* ARCHIMARSHAL ET ELEC *(Archmarshal and Elector).* The elaborate coat of arms, typical of German coins of this era, resulted from the frequent division and recombination of territory through inheritance and marriage, and the German custom of displaying every crest, shield, badge, or other device to which a ruler had claim.

Hungary, 1695 taler, Leopold I (1657–1705). Bewigged bust of the Emperor, LEOPOLDUS DG ROM IMP SA GE HV BO REX. *Double-headed crowned eagle,* ARCHIDVX AVS DVX BVR MAR MOR CO TYR *(Emperor of the Romans, ever august; King of Germany, Hungary, Bohemia; Archduke of Austria; Duke of Burgundy; Margrave of Moravia; Count of Tyrol).* The Hapsburgs, reigning family of Austria, also headed the Holy Roman Empire from 1438 until 1806. Over the centuries, they extended their rule to include many nations as indicated in the titles shown on this coin.

Switzerland, canton of Basel, undated taler of the eighteenth century. View of the city, spires of its eleventh century cathedral and the Rhine River, BASILEA. *Coat of arms,* DOMINE CONSERVA NOS IN PACE *(Lord, preserve us in peace).* Until 1850, Swiss coins were issued in the name of individual cantons. Some collectors specialize in these city-view coins.

Spanish America (Guatemala mint), 1769 8 reales, Charles III (1760–88). Pillars of Hercules and two hemispheres, VTRA QUE VNUM (Make both one). Spanish coats of arms, CAROLUS III DG HISPAN ET IND REX (King of Spain and the Indies). The first New World coinage came from the Spanish mints of Mexico and Central and South America. The 8-reales pieces were so common in Britain's American colonies that the United States dollar was based on this coin.

Brazil, 1814 960 reis, John, Prince Regent (1799–1816). Globe on cross, SUBQ SIGN NATA STAB (The land discovered under this sign shall prosper). Portuguese coat of arms, JOANNES DG PORT P REGENS ET BRAS D. Portugal was the second great colonial power in the Americas, with Brazil occupying nearly half of the South American continent. Brazil was a Portuguese colony until 1822, an empire until 1889, a republic since then.

France, 5 francs, Napoleon Bonaparte (1799–1815). Napoleon's rise to power can be read on his coins. The specimen at the top issued in year XI of the revolutionary calendar (A.D. 1803), shows him bare headed and with the title of first consul. By 1808, Napoleon's coins showed him wearing a laurel wreath and proclaimed him emperor. The reverse, however, continued to carry the inscription "Republic of France." By 1812, even the reverse read "Empire of France."

Bavaria, 1875 5 marks, Ludwig II (1864–86). The German Empire formed in 1871 reduced the number of coin-issuing states to twenty-five and established the 5-mark piece as the standard coin. The reverse designs were the same for all coins, but distinctive obverses were continued for the individual kingdoms, duchies, and cities.

China (Kiang Nan Province), undated dollar (struck 1897), Emperor Kuang Hsu (1875–1908). Chinese characters in the central part of the reverse read from right to left in Chinese fashion, "large money," and from top to bottom, "Kuang Hsu." Although the majority of crowns are from European countries, there is an extensive series of oriental crowns as well. Many of the Chinese dollars are available at comparatively low prices.

France, 1964 10 francs. Hercules group French dollar-size coins date back to 1641, but were halted in 1938. Beginning in 1964, however, France resumed striking large pieces in response to the demand of French citizens for a heavy silver coin. The face value of the new coin is approximately $2.00, but it is never seen in actual circulation.

Sierra Leone, 1964 1 leone. This African nation gained its independence in 1961 after more than a century as a British Crown Colony. Over the centuries, it has been a symbol of authority for a government to issue coins in its own name and many of the newly independent nations have followed this custom. The Sierra Leone crown-size piece was limited to 10,000 specimens, all of which were included in cased proof sets.

105

Multiple talers

Silver dollar-size coins became popular during the 16th century and as silver became more plentiful, even larger size multiple talers appeared. Struck on heavier, broader planchets, the multiples were usually the weight of two, three and even four normal talers. Many of these large coins commemorate battles and treaties, record weddings and deaths or mark years of high productivity of a particular mine. The multiples also served as a means of storing bullion and in time of war or other necessity, they were often called in by the local rulers.

Saxony, 1650 double taler of John George I. This issue marks the Peace of Westphalia which ended the Thirty Years' War.

Brunswick-Luneberg-Celle, 1654 triple taler. The obverse shows a free horse galloping above the city of Celle, seat of the duchy.

Great Britain, 1643 pound of Charles I (1625–49). Struck at the Oxford mint.

Denmark, undated double taler of Christian IV (1588–1648).

Panama, 1971 20 balboas. Head of Simon Bolivar, national arms on the reverse. This coin, marking the sesquicentennial of Central American independence, is the heaviest coin issued in modern times. It contains more than a quarter pound of sterling silver. These coins were produced through 1976, for the Republic of Panama by the private Franklin Mint in Pennsylvania. Although legal tender in Panama for their face value, it is not likely that many of these large, heavy pieces will actually be circulated.

NON-CIRCULATING LEGAL TENDER ISSUES

Coins struck especially for collectors are not new on the numismatic scene—nearly all official government proof coins, for example, are in this category. In England, minting special varieties of tradesmen's tokens for collectors was a common practice nearly two centuries ago. The last decade, however, has brought a tremendous growth in this kind of activity. Several private organizations, often in conjunction with recognized governments, are producing issues that are declared to be legal tender coins even though they are not intended for circulation and usually do not correspond to the denominations in actual use. These pieces are nearly all beautifully struck, their designs are attractive and they deal with popular subjects. Nevertheless, there is a great deal of controversy as to whether these constitute bona fide numismatic issues. They are, however, widely advertised and many collectors are buying them.

The first of the recently-issued, non-circulating coins was this 50 diners silver piece of Andorra, a tiny republic in the Pyrenees Mountains between France and Spain. The obverse depicts Charlemagne who is credited by tradition with having granted the country its independence in the days of the Frankish Empire. Regular issue French and Spanish coins are used in daily circulation.

The American astronauts and the moon flights and landings have
been the subject of several issues. This silver piece has been declared
legal tender for 10 riyals in the emirate of Fujairah.

This $1000 legal tender gold coin was issued by Hong Kong in 1980
to commemorate the "Year of the Monkey." Struck in 22 carat
gold, the coin measures 28.4mm in diameter and weighs 15.98 grams.
The monkey has been featured in Chinese art and legends for 2,000
years and has fascinated the Chinese for many centuries. (The
Hong Kong dollar is valued at approximately 20 cents U.S.)

TOKEN COLLECTING

Token collecting has long been accepted as a worthwhile branch of numismatics and in many ways tokens preserve for us a more intimate picture of their time than do the coins. Among the first American and British collectors, tokens were given at least as much attention as the regularly issued coins. On tokens we find contemporary portraits of noteworthy persons as well as the slogans and sentiments of the period. Another fascinating feature: the tradesmen's tokens show the wares of their time such as grinding stones and top hats. Thousands of varieties of tokens have been issued. Some were merely advertising pieces but many, released during coin shortages, were readily accepted as small change and their coinage ran up into millions of pieces.

U.S. "Hard Times" tokens issued in the period 1834–44 were the size of the then-current large cents. Many of the tokens were political, referring to President Andrew Jackson's fight against the United States Bank.

U.S. tokens of the Civil War period were of two principle types: patriotic tokens which carried a design or motto appropriate to the times or tradesmen's tokens with an advertising message. Some were close imitations of the contemporary Indian Head cent but carried the inscription "Not One Cent."

AUSTRALIA

CANADA

GREAT BRITAIN

GERMANY

A wide variety of tokens appeared in Germany during the period following World War I when all coins with intrinsic metal value virtually disappeared. To keep pace with the skyrocketing inflation, emergency token coins were inscribed with values which ran as high as a billion marks in one instance.

Among the many unusual substitutes for metal used during this period was porcelain. These porcelain coins issued by the state of Saxony were produced at Meissen, known for centuries as a center of the ceramics industry.

Encased postage stamps

One of the most unusual and interesting types of U.S. tokens was the encased postage stamp series used during the Civil War. For a brief period, the Federal government authorized the use of postage stamps as a medium of exchange. To preserve the stamps, a man by the name of Gault designed a brass case with a mica window to enclose them. Nearly all encased postage stamps carry merchant's advertising messages on the back of the case.

The greatest number of encased postage stamps used as currency appeared in Germany during the emergency period following World War I. Other nations that have used them are Argentina, Austria, Belgium, Czechoslovakia, Denmark, France, French Guinea, Greece, Italy, Ivory Coast, Madagascar, New Caledonia, Norway, Russia, Spain and Turkey. The last official issue was made during the Spanish Civil War.

116

SIEGE COINS

An older kind of emergency coinage (often called obsidional money) frequently appeared in times of war or revolutions. When money ran out in a beleagured city or province, silver plate was simply cut up in squares and stamped with official emblems and valuations.

Many of the siege coins were produced in the Netherlands during the 16th and 17th centuries where more than 250 towns were besieged in the running battle between the Spanish royalist forces and revolutionaries. These diamond-shaped, uniface pieces are 12½ stuivers issued by Groningen in 1672 and 2 sols struck in Breda in 1625.

This odd-shaped 7 gulden piece was cut from silverware by order of the governor of Julich when this German city was besieged by the Dutch in 1610.

Siege coins were struck at Newark during the English Civil War of 1642–49. The city supported Charles I and endured three sieges during the "Great Rebellion." These 30 and 9 pence specimens are from 1646.

The Dutch city of Leyden was besieged by the Spanish for more than a year in 1573–74. Nearly half of the population was carried off by plague and every last bit of food was eaten up. To provide a circulating currency, pages from church hymn books were glued together and pressed between dies. This piece was valued at 30 stuivers.

How Coins Are Made

Knowing a little about how coins are made—in earlier times as well as now—helps a collector to understand about such things as die varieties and flaws and especially about errors and mis-struck pieces.

Sometimes, due to such minute variations, flaws, cracks, errors, recutting, etc., it is possible to identify and distinguish between coins struck from different sets of dies even though the coins bear the same date and design. This is particularly true of the older coins made in the handcraft days before the mints were highly mechanized. Variations of this sort, known as die varieties, are the concern of collectors specializing in a given series.

DIE VARIETIES

To strike a coin, a pair of dies, obverse ("head") and reverse ("tail"), are required. For the design to stand up in relief on the finished coin, it must be cut (incused) into the die. Occasionally, a die will crack or chip while still in use. When this

Reverse die for an Edward III (1327–77) groat. Early coins were produced by hand-hammering. The dies were also produced by hand and no two were ever exactly alike.

Coin dies and punches from 17th and 18th century German mints.

happens the crack impresses itself on to the coins as a line, an unintentional addition to the design.

A chip in the die appears as a dot on the coin. Working the other way, waste material can clog up part of a die. When part of the die is filled in, that portion of the design (usually a letter or numeral) is not impressed on the coin.

The earliest U.S. coins for example were struck from dies each of which had been prepared entirely by the hands of a skilled workman. The complete design was engraved directly on to steel which was then hardened, making a die. Slight variations can be noted in the design on the coins produced from each succeeding set of dies. On the head of Liberty with flowing hair that appears on the 1795 half dimes, for example, coins from one die have her with six locks of hair while those from the other dies show seven. Similarly, on the silver dollars

These 1795 half dimes show (left) a die crack extending from RT in the legend across the hair and forehead to the ear and on to the first star at the lower left and (right) a mass of metal from a broken die nearly obliterating 4 stars at the right edge of the coin.

of 1795 there are varieties showing two leaves on the branch below the eagle's wing while other varieties show three leaves. A feature or a combination of features that makes it possible to differentiate between coins struck from one set of dies and the coins of all other dies of that date is said to be "diagnostic of the die."

In about 1795, with the introduction of the draped bust of Liberty on U.S. coins, punches or hubs were used for the major

(Left) Reverse of the 1795 U.S. silver dollar with two leaves below the eagle's wing and (right) with three leaves. The slight variation shows that they were struck from different dies even though both are dated 1795.

Master portrait punch for the gold 5 guineas of Charles II.

parts of the design such as the heads and the eagles, and there was no longer any variation in the design of these features. However, letters, numerals and stars were still punched in individually; it is possible to distinguish between dies by

Germanisches National-Museum, Nurnberg

Screw presses such as this were the standard coin striking machines
of the 17th and 18th centuries.

(Left) Wide-date, and (right) narrow-date cent of 1817. During this period, the stars and digits of the date were stamped individually into the dies. Note also that the left coin has 13 stars, the right one 15 stars.

comparing the relative size and position of these portions of the design.

About 1838, the time the Seated Liberty figure came into use on U.S. coins, the complete design except for the date and mint mark was put into each working die from one master hub. Occasionally we see a variation in the size or placement of the digits in the date or the mint letter, but it is not possible to distinguish between many of the dies. Modern coins are struck from dies prepared from a master hub that even includes the date.

(Left) master punch, (right) working die for obverse of Elizabeth II (1952–) coins.

MODERN COIN PRODUCTION

Even in the most modern mints, coins are made today in much the same way they have been produced since steam power was first applied to minting nearly two centuries ago. The basic idea, that of impressing blank pieces of metal between two dies, dates back to the time of the ancient Greeks. Many of the world's mints have guided tours or observation windows for visitors. Seeing a mint in operation is a great treat for anyone interested in coins.

British Crown Copyright, reproduced by permission of the Deputy Master of the Royal Mint

New coin designs are first prepared as large plaster models. An electrotype copy is made from this and placed on a reducing machine which cuts a master punch in actual coin size by means of a tracer that runs over the face of the model. The master punch which has the features of the design in relief is used to sink working dies with the features incuse.

In the first stage of the actual coining process, the proper proportions of the constituent metals are placed in melting furnaces (above) where they are mixed together. The molten metal is poured out into moulds which produce rectangular bars. These bars are then passed through rolling mills (below) which flatten them into strips of proper thickness.

125

In the next stage of production, cutting machines punch blank planchets out of the metal strips (above) and the edges are turned up, making a rim on each side of the planchet to protect the design from wear. The planchets then pass through an annealing furnace (below) to soften them for striking.

The final step in the coining process is the impression of the design onto the blank planchets. The photograph above shows the press room at the old Royal Mint on Tower Hill in London. The picture below shows the coinage room of the new mint at Llantrisant, Wales, where mechanical equipment feeds blanks to six lines of presses and collects the finished coins.

127

Planchets and coins are inspected at all stages of production. The view above, at the private The Mint, Birmingham, Ltd., shows rows of high speed electrical presses in operation with coiners spot-checking the newly struck coins. The photograph below, at the Royal Australian Mint in Canberra, shows newly minted coins on a conveyor belt moving past the final inspection station.

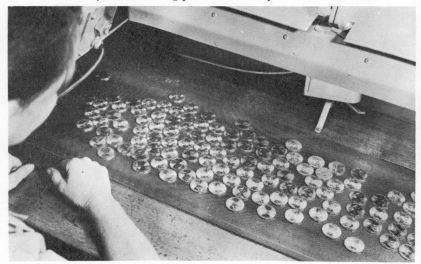

ODDITIES AND ERRORS

Errors can occur at several steps in the coining process and varieties can be created in preparing the dies. The following pages tell about the most interesting kinds of oddities and provides an explanation of how they come about.

Until a few years ago, collectors of U.S. looked for the "plain," "D," and "S" mint issues of each year and except for obvious overdates and changes of design, that was it.

Oddity collectors tend to give their discoveries fanciful names. This "cracked skull" cent is so named because of the prominent die breaks across Lincoln's head.

Now, however, collectors examine coins with magnifying glasses, even microscopes, searching for new varieties.

Strange terms like "bugs-bunny" half dollars, "adam's apple" quarters, "fanged" Roosevelt dimes, double-profile nickels, "cracked-skull" and "dagger-in-back" Lincoln cents have found their way into U.S. numismatics lately. Collectors in other countries are now looking for mint errors on their coins.

Varieties, oddities and errors give collectors something more to look for. New issues alone are not enough to sustain interest in a collection. And as date and mint-mark sets approach completion, it can be a long time between "finds" unless you look for varieties too.

Interest in varieties causes collectors to study their coins, to inquire about how they are made and how varieties and errors come about. You are sure to hear more soon about varieties, as they are added to catalogue listings and given spaces in albums. They are worth knowing about, since a growing demand for this kind of material will definitely result in significant price increases.

How they happen

Here are the kinds of errors and how they happen.

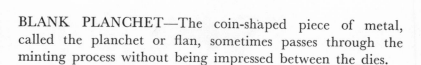

This blank nickel planchet slipped past the dies without having the design impressed. Note, however, that it did go through a milling machine which thickened or "upset" the edge.

BLANK PLANCHET—The coin-shaped piece of metal, called the planchet or flan, sometimes passes through the minting process without being impressed between the dies.

CLIPPED PLANCHET—The planchets are punched out of a strip of metal passing through a cutting machine. Imperfect planchets with a circular "bite" are the result of successive

130

punches made too close together. A "straight-edge" planchet would come from a punch too close to the end of the strip. These cutting errors are fairly common and since they can easily be simulated outside the mint they have little premium value.

OFF-CENTRED COIN—If the planchet is not properly centred between the dies, only a portion of the design appears on the coin. Sometimes the planchet is nearly blank with just a small part of the design showing.

DOUBLE-STRUCK COIN—If the coin is not ejected properly after being struck, a second impression is made on the same planchet. The second impression is frequently off centred as well.

This picture shows a bronze planchet intended for a Lincoln cent that has been impressed with the Jefferson nickel design. The lettering runs off the edge of the coin since the copper planchet is smaller than the nickel dies.

OFF-METAL COIN—These occur when a planchet intended for a coin in one metal is inadvertently mixed with planchets of another metal. Silver U.S. cents struck on dime planchets are the variety most often found. Under present U.S. laws, it is illegal to hold this kind of error. Technically, no coin is legal

131

until it is authorized and issued for circulation. Even then it is illegal unless it corresponds in all respects to the authorization. Cents, of course, are not authorized in silver.

Inadvertent mixing of planchets also explains wrong-size coins, such as a quarter struck on a dime planchet. Off-metal coins are scarce and would probably be worth $75–$125 (£50–£83) if they could be legally traded.

OVERSIZE COIN—A thinner, oversize "pancake" coin with rounded edges occurs when the collar does not contain the coin properly.

A cracked die reveals itself as a raised line on the coins struck from it. This nickel (enlarged) shows a die break line extending across all four legs of the buffalo. Nickel is the least malleable of the coinage metals and is very hard on dies.

DIE BREAK—A break or crack in the working die causes a similar raised mark on the surface of the coin (connected letters, etc.).

FILLED DIE—If part of a die fills up with metal scraps or other material, that portion does not impress itself on the coins, resulting in missing letters, numbers, etc.

BROCKAGE—A coin showing the same design on both sides; one perfectly struck, the other an incuse mirror image. Caused by the preceding coin sticking to one of the dies.

LAMINATED PLANCHET—If the planchet metal is not properly annealed (softened and made less brittle), pieces of metal strip off or peel away.

DOUBLE DIE, DOUBLE PROFILE, DOUBLE LETTERS or DATE—If the master die shifts or bounces between punches into a working die, all of the coins struck from that die will show a double impression of the design. A double strike can occur too if a coin sticks in the die and is impressed a second time. If it shifts the tiniest fraction between impressions, at least part of the design will be doubled. One impression is almost a "shadow" of the other. All of a coin's design does not appear doubled in these situations; the second strike wipes out or hides the first strike on some parts of the coin.

DOUBLE MINT MARK—Mint letters are struck by hand into the die before it goes out to the branch mint. If the workman shifts his punch at all between blows, the die will have a doubly-impressed mint letter. Coins struck with such a die will show a double mint mark.

Until 1965, all U.S. coins by law had to be struck from dies showing the correct year of issue. In the early days of the mint, the die sinkers punched the new date over the old on dies that were still serviceable at the end of the year. This 1802 silver dollar clearly shows the numeral 2 in the date punched in over the 1.

OVERDATE—Infrequently, through error or emergency need for coins, older dies have been stamped over with the current date. The earlier numeral shows up below the new one (such as a 2 on top of a 1 which looks a little like a dollar sign). OVERSTRUCK MINT MARK—This is a situation similar to an overdate. If a workman strikes a coin first with the wrong punch and then corrects his error, a trace of the first letter may appear. When there was more than one branch mint, the mint letter on a die prepared for one could be restamped and sent to a different branch.

RECUT DATE OR LETTER—Worn dies can be reconditioned for sharper impressions by recutting worn letters or numerals. The recut portion shows a faint outline.

A recent widely publicized die variation is in the 1960 cent. (Left) Large-date variety. The top of the "9" extends above "1," "6" has a long tail and the "0" is decidedly round. (Right) Small-date variety.

LARGE AND SMALL DATES, MICROSCOPIC MINT MARKS, etc.—These varieties are relative to each other. They occur when two sets of punches of different sizes are used in preparing dies or when there is a change in the master die during the course of the year.

Collecting Ancient Coins

THE REMARKABLE age of the Greek and Roman coins in itself makes these pieces appealing to experienced collectors and beginners alike. The beauty of workmanship and the artistry of style is readily apparent. The ancient coins are essential to any comprehensive numismatic study as all subsequent coinages are to some extent based on the ancient series.

This silver dekadrachm of the Greek city-state of Syracuse (c. 400 B.C.) is one of the most beautiful and sought-after of all ancient coins. Obverse: head of Persephone. Reverse: charioteer driving a *quadriga*, with a winged figure, Victory, flying above the chariot.

The people of the ancient world were great hoarders. There were no banks as we know them today, so coins were often buried in the ground or sealed up in walls. Deposits of ancient coins are still being dug up today and there are many hoards still to be found. Because of these finds, many coins of the Greeks and Romans are not nearly as scarce or expensive as might be expected in relation to their antiquity.

GREEK COINS

The Greek people were the first to utilize coins in the form we think of—portable objects, reasonably round and flat, of standard weight and fineness, having an intrinsic value of precious metal.

These "turtle" coins of Aegina are among the first known coinages. They date back to about 650 B.C.

The very earliest coins were made about 700 B.C. by the kingdom of Lydia (in what is Turkey on our maps today) followed soon after by the turtle coins of Aegina (a Greek island). The Persians had a large coinage by the 6th century B.C. and their silver siglos were the first coins to be widely circulated. These first coins had designs on one side only, the reverse having only "incuse squares" from the anvil. The later coins have designs on both sides, often in beautiful high relief.

Stater
c. 150 B.C.

Tetradrachm
c. 450 B.C.

Coins of Athens can be recognized by the head of Athena, Goddess of wisdom, or by the owl, emblem of wisdom.

Display of Greek coins

The Greek coins range in size from the tiny hemiobols to large, thick dekadrachms. Coins even of the same denomination vary greatly in size. This lack of uniformity makes it difficult to display a collection in the usual manner. Most specialists in the Greek series keep their coins in the 2″ × 2″ coin envelopes or in trays with separate compartments for each coin. It is useful to have at hand as much information about each coin as possible. The basic attribution for a Greek coin consists of the following data:

1. Name of city or state that issued the coin (also its name and location on present-day maps).

2. Date or period of issue.

3. Identification of figures and devices on obverse and reverse (the name of the ruler if a regal coin).

4. Denomination and metal.

 The Greek coins were struck by hand with a hammer, a punch and an anvil. Consequently, they are usually irregular in shape.

Ancient coins often cannot be dated as precisely as more modern issues. Most Greek coins, however, can be assigned reasonably accurate dates of issue that scholars have arrived at by studying the style, symbols and workmanship of the coins.

No two ancient coins are ever precisely alike. The coins were created one at a time by workmen using only an anvil, punch and mallet. Size and shape vary greatly because the lump of metal would spread out differently each time. Many ancient coins are weakly struck or off mark. Sometimes more than one blow from the mallet was required to attain the desired relief and detail. If the punch slipped a little between blows, "double struck" coins occurred. This lack of uniformity is one of the charms of the ancient coinages.

It is always desirable to possess a coin in the finest possible condition, but it is a rewarding and pleasant experience to own an ancient coin in any condition. Condition is a very important factor in the value of an ancient Greek coin. A coin in superb condition may easily cost ten times as much as the same item in lesser but still presentable condition. The collector who demands only the finest can be satisfied but the collector of modest means need not be discouraged either. Actually, the chances of significant historical participation are greater for worn coins than for those in better condition.

Athenian dekadrachm c. 480 B.C. and triobol (½ drachm) c. 450 B.C. Compare size with the tetradrachm shown on page 136.

Greek coin denominations varied greatly over the years and in different localities. The silver coins were struck primarily on the basis of a unit designated as a "drachm." Multiples of the drachm were the rare dekadrachm (10), the widely used tetradrachm (4), and the didrachm (2). Smaller silver pieces were based on the "obol," the sixth part of a drachm. Values found are the triobol (3 obols or $\frac{1}{2}$ drachm), the diobol (2), the trihemiobol ($1\frac{1}{2}$), the obol itself and the hemiobol ($\frac{1}{2}$). Another often-encountered coin is the silver "stater." The older coins were often designated as staters but this value also varied from issue to issue.

The prices for the larger coins are generally higher than for the smaller pieces. The large coins provide space for more artistic expression and are generally found in better condition.

(Left) Tetradrachm of Carthage. (Right) Silver stater of Corinth, c. 400 B.C. with head of Athena and Pegasus, the mythological flying horse.

Silver didrachm of Tarentum, c.350 B.C. Many ancient coins can be recognized by their designs. The Tarentines were renowned as horsemen, and a rider is often a mark of their coinage.

Head of Alexander the Great on Egyptian tetradrachm of Ptolemy I.

Silver tetradrachm of Ptolemy I with his own likeness, c. 300 B.C.

Base silver tetradrachm of Cleopatra of Egypt, 51–30 B.C.

A study of these coins is most enjoyable to students of history. Many of the basic ideas of Western thought have their roots in the time and places represented by these coins.

ROMAN COINS

The traditional date of the founding of Rome is 753 B.C. By about 300 B.C., Rome was supreme in Italy and the first series of true Roman coins made their appearance. This was a series of heavy cast pieces known as the "aes grave" or "heavy bronze." The largest coin was an "as" and weighed several ounces. The obverse bears the head of Janus, the god of beginnings and endings. The reverse shows the prow of a ship and a mark of value. The lower values each have the head of a different god or goddess but the ship's prow reverse is common to all.

Bronze "as" of the Roman Republic. These early bronze coins were cast, not struck from dies.

Silver coins came into use about the time of the First Punic War in 264 B.C. The principal coin was the well-known denarius with the head of the goddess Roma wearing a winged helmet. The reverse shows the Dioscuri, the Heavenly twins—

Standard silver denarius of the Roman Republic. Obverse: helmeted head of the goddess Roma. Reverse: the Dioscuri (the heavenly twins—Castor and Pollux).

Castor and Pollux. They were credited with having led the Roman army to victory and their cult was very popular among the Romans at the time the denarius was introduced. Many different types were issued later as the coin became more popularly used.

Roman Imperial coinage

The coinage of the Empire begins in 27 B.C. when Octavian became Emperor of Rome, taking the name of Caesar Augustus. It lasted until the fall of the emperor Romulus Augustulus in A.D. 476.

During these five centuries of coinage, many different denominations, sizes and types of coins were used. With very few exceptions, however, the coins all show the head and titles of the reigning emperor. The reverses generally show a Roman deity or a personification, although a few coins have only inscriptions.

Denarius of Augustus, the first Roman emperor. This was the standard silver coin of the empire.

Bronze sestertius of Emperor Nero (54–68 A.D.). The large sestertii are the most attractive of all the Roman coins and choice condition specimens are greatly sought after.

The most popular type of Roman Imperial coin collection is one with coins representing as many different rulers as possible. With the exception of a few emperors who held power for just a few days or months, each reign can be represented by some coin at modest cost. Coins were also sometimes struck showing the empress; the emperor's children; his parents; in one case, his grandmother; his adopted heir.

This sestertius shows Sabina, the wife of Hadrian (117–138).

In some respects, the reverses of the Roman coins are more interesting, varied and significant historically than the obverses which nearly always show a bust of the ruler or member of his family. These coins circulated throughout the empire which was made up of many diverse groups of people and thus had great propaganda value. The coinage proclaimed the universality of Roman law and rule and was designed to inspire loyalty to the empire. The reverse designs fall into three main

Reverse of a sestertius of Titus (79–81 A.D.) shows the Colosseum. Historians have learned a great deal about Roman buildings and customs by studying coins.

groups: gods and goddesses; allegorical personifications; designs relating to the emperor or to events in the empire.

There is a great variety of types referring to deeds of the emperor. His entries into cities, journeys through the provinces, victories and triumphs, presents to the people and army and happy events in the Imperial family are all recorded. Coins were issued showing buildings such as the Circus Maximus, the Colosseum, temples, bridges, aqueducts, etc.

Roman coins often represent actions or ideas personified, that is, in human form. (Left) Libertas—liberty or freedom, holding a pileus, a pointed cap of liberty, similar to the one that appears on early United States coins. (Middle) Pietas—piety or dutifulness, holding a patera, a sacrificial bowl, and a sceptre. (Right) Moneta—money or minting, holding a scale and cornucopia—of particular interest to numismatists.

143

Attribution of Roman coins

The basic attribution for a Roman coin consists of the following data:

1. Name of the emperor under whom issued if an Imperial coin or the moneyer if a family coin of the Republic.

2. Date of issue as closely as can be determined.

3. A translation of the obverse and reverse legends.

4. Identification of the figures and devices and their significance if known.

5. Denomination and metal.

Because of the range of sizes in the various denominations and the lack of uniformity even of different specimens of the same denomination, ancient Roman coins are most easily kept and stored in standard 2″ × 2″ coin envelopes which also allow the collector to have information about each coin right at hand.

Condition of Roman coins

Most Roman coins circulated extensively during their period of use in ancient times. Consequently, many of them that have come down to us are not in as fine a state of preservation as the numismatist might desire. On the other hand, part of the charm of having an ancient coin is the consideration of where and by whom it may have been used in its earlier days.

Some of the bronze coins, over the years, have taken on a lustrous, smooth, green coating called "patina." Collectors of this series usually consider "patinated" pieces especially desirable. The new collector may or may not care for patinated pieces but is cautioned not to refer to the condition as a blemish in the presence of experienced collectors.

Occasionally the early Republican denarii are encountered with a notched or "serrated" edge. This was a device intended to discourage counterfeiting and is not an imperfection.

Coin Identification

THE FIRST STEP toward identifying a coin is to determine its country of origin. During the past hundred years alone, more than three hundred different nations, states, colonies, and cities have issued distinctive coins. And the farther back we go, the more diverse the coin issues become. Literally hundreds of areas and cities that are now absorbed into modern nations were once independent or under different authority and, as such, issued coins under their own names. Although the authority that produced the coin may no longer exist, many coins have survived even from centuries ago and, the collector's aim is to attribute them as nearly as possible to the locality that produced them. In most cases, the inscriptions on the coins themselves are the means of accurate identification based on the system of "key words" explained in the following pages.

MODERN COINS

Most modern world coins are easy to attribute. A sizable proportion of them, including those from most of the British colonies and Commonwealth nations (but *not* Britain itself) show the name of the issuing country in English. Then, too, many countries are known in English by the same name as in their native languages. Spanish is the official language in most of Central and South America, but you will recognize coins of Argentina, Bolivia, Chile, Columbia, Costa Rica, Cuba, Ecuador, Guatemala, Honduras, Nicaragua, Panama, Paraguay, Peru, El Salvador, Uruguay, Venezuela, and others right

| Colombia | Haiti | Timor |

The names of many countries are exactly the same in English as in the language of the country itself, which makes identification easy.

away because we use their Spanish names when we speak and write English. The same is true also of some other coin-issuing states, such as Haiti, Madagascar, Mali, and Timor, that use languages besides Spanish. To identify these coins, all you need to know is your geography so that you recognize the country name when you see it.

Another large group of countries issues coins on which the name in the native language is close enough to English for you to guess with some confidence where they are from. Here are

Czechoslovakia (CESKOSLOVENSKA)   Norway (NORGE)

Even when country names are not exactly the same as English, they are often so similar that a collector can easily guess where a coin is from. If you have any doubts, however, check the key word in the identifier list.

some foreign country names from the Coin Finder list which you will probably recognize right away: Belgique (Belgium), Brasil (Brazil), Cabo Verde (Cape Verde), Ceskoslovenska (Czechoslovakia), España (Spain), Filipinas (Philippines), Island (Iceland), Kibris (Cyprus), Norge (Norway), Polska (Poland), Sverige (Sweden). If you want to double-check your guesswork on such coins, just look up the names in the list of key words that follows for verification (or correction) of your deduction.

Other countries issue coins that are not so easily identified until you know certain key words. You may need help, at least the first time, to know that "Deutsches Reich" is Germany, "Helvetia" is Switzerland, and "Magyar" is Hungary. It is almost certain you will not recognize "Euzkadi" as the Viscayan Republic, "Suomi" as Finland, or "Shqipni" as Albania. Some of these key words are written on coins with the Greek or Cyrillic alphabets and can only be appoximated using English characters. These words, such as PYbAb on Russian coins or

Finland (SUOMEN)   Russia (CCCP)

Some countries' coins are not so easily identified without a little detective work. The key words, however, will give you the information you want. Coin denominations are not usually diagnostic because cents, francs, etc., are used in so many parts of the world. In the case of the coins illustrated, however, you will find both PENNIA and KOIIEEK (kopeck) in the identifier section as they are used only in Finland and Russia, respectively.

CBbNJA on Serbian coins are preceded by an asterisk (*) in the key-word list.

You may also encounter coins from Moslem and oriental countries which do not have any recognizable words. Compare these coins with the illustrations in the Visual Identification section following the key-word listing. Watch especially for the key elements of the designs shown on the pictures.

A large proportion of the coins issued in the past hundred and fifty years are from British, French, and Portuguese colonies. Be sure to read the complete inscription on coins that

*Libya, 1965
50 milliemes*

A few modern coins from Moslem and oriental countries do not show the name of the issuing nation in recognizable letters. Even these can be identified, however, by comparing them with the illustrations in the Visual Identification section.

seem to be from Britain, France, or Portugal to determine whether they are from the country itself or one of the colonies.

As mentioned earlier, coins of Great Britain do not show the name of the country in English. Except for the denomination, British coin inscriptions are in Latin. The key word in identifying them is BRITANNIARUM (of Britain), although on most recent issues, it is abbreviated to BRITT. or even BR.

When you have an unknown foreign coin, study its design and inscriptions for clues to its identity. Check first of all to see whether the name appears anywhere in English or is close enough to English to be recognizable. Be sure not to pass over the name of some small colony or new nation without realizing it is the very name you are seeking. If reading the inscription on a coin doesn't tell you what country it is from, you'll have to find the key word or design element in the tables that follow. Pick the word that looks most promising and look it up. If you find it listed, the table will give you the name of the issuing country, plus the heading under which you will likely find the coin described in standard coin catalogs, as for example, BRAUNSCHWEIG—Brunswick (Germany). If the word you choose first isn't listed, keep trying until you find one that is. Generally, words such as "republic," "colony," "king," and their foreign equivalents and popular denominations like "cent" and "shilling" are no help—being common to so many coins, they are not diagnostic in identification. Words that seem unusual are likely to be the distinctive key words.

Rwanda, 1964
5 francs, President
Gregoire Kayibanda

The key word to identifying this coin is "RWANDA," the name of an African nation independent since 1962. You will find Rwanda listed in the table of contents of any up-to-date coin catalog, a list you should check occasionally to familiarize yourself with the names of coin-issuing countries.

COINS BEFORE 1800

Choosing the year 1800 as a pivotal point in world coinage is strictly arbitrary, as changes in coinage practice occurred at different times in different parts of the world. Yet, from the standpoint of coin identification, there are three factors to bear in mind in regard to coins issued before 1800.

First, nearly all legends on pre-1800 coins were in Latin and many of the words were engraved in abbreviated form. On small-size coins of rulers with long titles, the legends are sometimes abbreviated to the point of being little more than a string of initials.

Second, the republics we know today had not come into existence by 1800 and nearly every coin was issued in the name of an emperor, king, duke, or other noble. The sovereign's name, especially if the piece is dated, can be very useful in identifying a coin. By referring to a biographical dictionary or dated lists of rulers, you can often verify or add to your supposition about a coin. The key words on the coin illustrated are: POL, SIGISMUN, 99. Checking POL in the Identifier section will refer you to Poland. Consulting a coin catalog showing older

Poland, 1599 6 groschen, Sigismund III (1587–1632), SIGISMVN III DG REX POL M D L (*Sigismund III by the Grace of God King of Poland, Grand Duke of Lithuania*). GROS ARGEN SEX REG POLONI 99 (*6 silver groschen of the Polish kingdom*).

coins, a dated list of Polish kings, or a biographical reference under SIGISMUND will tell you that Sigismund III was indeed King of Poland from 1587 to 1632, thereby confirming your identification of the coin and adding to your attribution by telling you that the "99" must be specifically 1599.

Finally, a great many states, provinces, etc., that were later consolidated, were still issuing independent coinages, as for example, the provinces of The Netherlands—Gelderland, Holland, Overijssel, Utrecht, West Frisia, and Zeeland.

Netherlands, 1740 doit of the province of Holland

Netherlands, 1739 doit of the city of Utrecht

Coins of the Middle Ages are more difficult to identify than those struck after 1500, mainly because the legends are so often blurry or even partially illegible. The greatest problem for beginners is the recognition of letters in their medieval forms. The sample alphabets shown will acquaint you with the styles of lettering encountered on old coins. The important points to remember are that the letter U is invariably shown as a V, that J is shown as I, that letters are sometimes reversed (especially N's and C's), and that two letters are sometimes joined into one (ligated) such as AE. Be careful not to confuse B's and E's, H's and N's, and K's and R's, G's and 6's, which look very much alike if not sharply engraved.

151

During the Middle Ages all coins were inscribed with the Latin names of the towns and cities issuing them. To further complicate identification, these names were usually in abbreviated form. The earlier issues show only words, monograms, and crude designs. By the thirteenth century, however, as larger-size coins came into use, representations of saints, rulers, and coats of arms began to appear. The key to attribution, however, is still the legend. When referring to the Identifier section, remember that the key word on your coin may be in shorter form than shown in the table or spelled somewhat differently, depending upon the form. Occasionally letters are repeated in words such as TVVCIVM instead of just TVCIVM, the Latin word for Deutz, one of the mint cities of Cologne in Germany.

Cologne, gros tournois, Archbishop Walram (1332–49), WALRAM ARCHIEPCS COLONIE (Walram, Archbishop of Cologne). MONETA TVVCIEN (money of Deutz, mint of Cologne). XPC VICIT XPC REGNAT XPC IMPERAT (Christ conquers, Christ reigns, Christ commands).

The starting point of the legend is often marked with a small cross. The ruler's name nearly always comes first in its Latin form, abbreviated more often than not. The name is usually followed by DG (Dei Gratia—by the Grace of God) and the ruler's title (REX, DVX, COMES, EPIS—King, Duke, Count, Bishop). The ruler's title is followed by the names of his domains, also in abbreviated Latin. The territories are usually listed in order of importance. In attributing coins struck by foreign rulers for territories over which they had jurisdiction, allot them to the area in which the coins were intended to circulate. On their coins, many monarchs claimed sovereignty to territory long after the fact. Lengthy legends sometimes start on the obverse and continue on to the reverse of a coin. The reverse also often carries the name of the specific mint city (MONETA NOVA CIVIT IMPER TREMONIENSIS—New Money of the Imperial City of Tremonia—Dortmund, Germany). On larger coins, we often find religious mottoes as part of the reverse inscription (XPS REGNAT XPS IMPERAT XPS VINCIT—Christ reigns, Christ commands, Christ conquers).

Coin dates

Dated coins are much easier to locate in catalogs and the dates are often helpful in verifying a coin's attribution. Dates on coins came into general use about 1500, although many coins struck later are not dated. A few coins dated according to the Christian era are known from the late fourteenth century. The earliest dates are shown in Roman numerals. Arabic numeral dates did not appear until a century later, toward the end of the fifteenth century, the earliest known being 1484.

Imperial city of Aachen (Aix-la-Chapelle), 1375 groschen. Bust of Charlemagne, KAROLVS MAGNVS IMPERAT. XC VINCT XC REGN ANO DNI MCCCLXXV, MONETA IVNGHEIT *(Jungheit, mint of Aachen).*

Austria, 1484 ½ guldengroschen, Sigismund (1439–96), SIGIS-MVNDVS ARCHDVX AVSTRIE.

The Moslem calendar

Some very modern-looking coins carry dates in the 1300's, but these are from Moslem countries dated according to the Mohammedan calendar, which begins with their year 1, equivalent to our year 622 A.D. The year 622 is the date of Mohammed's flight or "Hegira" from Mecca; the Moslems number their years from this point. Moslem dates are given as A.H., meaning "After Hegira." To convert Moslem dates into Christian-era dates, a small computation is necessary because the Mohammedan calendar is based on a lunar year of 354 days

Morocco, 5 mazunas of A.H. 1321, the Moslem date equivalent to 1903 A.D.

rather than our solar year of 365 days. To convert Mohammedan (A.H.) into Christian (A.D.) dates, it is necessary to deduct
3 per cent from the A.H. date (compensation for the difference
in length of years) and add 622 to arrive at the A.D. equivalent.
Thus, a coin of Morocco dated 1321 was actually struck in 1903
according to our method of reckoning (1321 minus 3 per cent,
or roughly 40, plus 622 equals 1903). These A.H. date coins
turn up fairly regularly, and to avoid being fooled into thinking
you have a coin that is very much older than is actually the
case, bear in mind that the earliest Arabic-numeral full-dated
coin of the Christian era is from 1484.

Nuremburg, 1648 ⅓ taler klippe. Lamb, CHRISTO DUCE
VERBO LUCE *(Christ, the leader, the Word, the Light). Arms,*
est VbI DVX IesVs paX VICto Marte gVbernat *(Where Jesus
is the leader, war is conquered and Peace restored).*

The legend on the reverse of this coin is in the form of a
chronogram, an inscription in which certain letters, more
prominent than the others, express the date in Roman numerals when put together in the proper order. (In this case
we have 1M, 1D, 1C, 2X's, 5V's, 3I's = 1648.)

The same identification procedure using key words can be followed for nearly all coins. Many of the illustrations in this book are accompanied by captions that give the full legends as they appear on the coins. For practice, try identifying them using the pictures and legends alone. The following list of commonly used Latin words, names, and phrases will help you to understand the complete inscriptions on coins of this era.

Latin Words Used in Coin Legends

ABBAS — Abbot
ABBATISSA — Abbess
ADVOCATVS — Bailiff
ANNO — Year
ARCHIDVX — Archduke
ARCHIEPISCOPVS — Archbishop
ARGENTEA — of silver
AVREA — of gold
CASTRI — Castle
CIVITAS — City
CIVITAS IMPERIVM — Imperial (Free) City
CIVITAS LIBERVM — Free City
COMES — Count
D(EI) G(RATIA) — by the Grace of God
DOMINVS — Lord
DVCATVM — Duchy
DVX — Duke
ELECTOR — Elector of the Holy Roman Empire
EPISCOPVS — Bishop
ET — and
FID(EI) DE(FENSOR) — Defender of the Faith
IMPERATOR — Emperor
MAGISTER — Master
MAGNVS — Grand
MAGNVS DVX — Grand Duke
MARCHIO — Margrave
MONETA — Coin
MON(ETA) NOV(A) ARG(ENTA) — New silver coin
NOVA — New

PAX — Peace
PRINCEPS — Prince
REGINA — Queen
REIPVBLICA — Republic
REX — King
ROM(ANVM) IMP(ERATOR) — Roman Emperor
S(ACRVM) R(OMANVM) I(MPERIVM) — Holy
　　Roman Empire
S(EMPER) A(VGVSTVS) — Always magnificent
TVTOR — Regent
VICE COMES — Viscount
VRBS — City
Z — and

Latin Forms of Monarch's Names

ADOLPHVS — Adolph
ALFONSVS — Alfonso
ALBERTVS — Albert
BENEDICTVS — Benedict
CAROLVS — Charles
DIONIS — Denis
EDWARDVS — Edward
ERNESTVS — Ernest
FERNANDVS — Ferdinand
FRIDERICVS — Frederick
GEORGIVS — George
GVILLEIMVS — William
HENRICVS — Henry
HLVDOVVICVS — Louis
IACOBVS — James
IOHANNES — John
IOSEPHVS — Joseph
LUDOVICVS – Louis
PAVLVS — Paul
PETRVS — Peter
PHILLIPVS (PHS) — Philip
RAIMVNDO — Raymond
RENATVS — René
RICARDVS — Richard
ROBERTVS — Robert
RVDOLPHVS — Rudolph

INSCRIPTIONS ON COINS

Words written with the Greek or Cyrillic alphabets can only be approximated when using English characters. These words are preceded by an asterisk (*) in the following key-word list.

AARGAU — Argau (Switzerland)
ACVNVM — Ancona (Italy)
*AEBA — Bulgaria
*AENTA — Crete, Greece
AFRICA PORTUGUEZA — Angola
AFRIQUE DE L'OUEST — West African States
AFRIQUE EQUATORIALE FRANÇAISE — French Equatorial Africa
AFRIQUE OCCIDENTALE FRANÇAISE — French West Africa
AFRIQUE ORIENTALE — Mozambique
AGLIA — England (Great Britain)
AGRIPPINA — Cologne (Germany)
AGVIS — Aachen (Germany)
AICHSTADIVM — Eichstadt (Germany)
AISSINDIA — Essen (Germany)
ALGARBIORUM — Algarve (Portugal)
ALGERIE — Algeria
ALOSTENSIS — Alost (Flanders — Belgium)
ALSATIA — Alsace (Germany)
ALWAR — India (Native State)
AMBIANIS — Amiens (France)
AMERICA CENTRAL — Costa Rica
ANDEGAVIS — Anjou (France)
ANDVSIENSIS — Anduse (France)
ANGL — Great Britain
ANH — Anhalt (Germany)
*ANHAPA — Serbia, Yugoslavia
AN HWEI — China
ANTILLEN — Netherlands Antilles
ANTVVP — Antwerp (Brabant — Belgium)
ANVERS — Antwerp (Brabant — Belgium)
*APAXMAI — Greece

Greece

Portugal

Great Britain

APOSTOLORVM PRINCEPS — Papal States (Italy)
APPENZELL — Switzerland
AQVENSIS — Aachen (Germany)
AQVIS — Aachen (Germany)
AQVITANIA — Aquitaine (France)
ARAGONE — Aragon (Spain)
ARAVSID — Orange (France)
ARENBERGAE — Arenberg (Germany)
ARGAU — Switzerland

Papal States

ARGENTORATVM — Strasbourg (France)
ARGOVIA — Argau (Switzerland)
ASSINDIA — Essen (Germany)
ASTENSIS — Asti (Italy)
AUSTRIAE — Austria
AVGVSTAS VINDILICORVM — Augsburg (Germany)
AVINIO — Avignon (France)
AVRASIGE — Orange (France)
AVRELIANVS — Orleans (France)
AVTIOCERCI — Auxerre (France)
BAD — Baden (Germany)
BAHAWALPUR — India (Native State)
BALEARES — Balearic Isles (Spain)
BAM — Bamberg (Germany)
BANK DEUTSCHER LÄNDER
  — Germany (Western Zone)
BARCANONA — Barcelona (Spain)
BARCINO — Barcelona (Spain)
BARRI — Bar (Lorraine — France)
BAS CANADA — Quebec (Canada)
BASILEA — Basel (Switzerland)
BAV — Bavaria (Germany)
BAYERN — Bavaria (Germany)
*BbATAPNR — Bulgaria
BELGEN — Belgium
BELGES — Belgium
BELGIE — Belgium
BELGIQUE — Belgium
BELGISCH CONGO — Belgian Congo
BERNENSIS — Berne (Switzerland)
BIKANIR — India (Native State)
BISONTIVM — Besançon (France)

Basel

Berne

159

BITERIS — Beziers (France)
BITVRICES — Bourges (France)
BLEDONIS — Beldo (France)
BLESIS — Blois (France)
BOGOTA — Colombia
BOHEM — Bohemia (Austria)
BOHMEN UND MÄHREN — Bohemia & Moravia
   (Czechoslovakia)

Bohemia-Moravia

BOLIVIANA — Bolivia
BOLVNENE — Boulogne (France)
BONNENSIS — Bonn (Cologne — Germany)
BONONIA — Bologna (Italy)
BORNEO — British North Borneo
BORUSSORUM — Prussia (Germany)
BRAB — Brabant (Belgium)
BRABANTIE — Brabant (Belgium)
BRAND — Brandenburg (Germany)
BRASIL — Brazil
BRASILLIAE — Brazil

Bologna

BRAUNSCHWEIG — Brunswick (Germany)
BREGA — Brieg (Silesia — Austria)
BREMENSIS — Bremen (Germany)
BR ET LUN — Brunswick (Germany)
BRITANNIARUM — Great Britain
BRITANNIE — Brittany (France)
BRITT — Great Britain

Brunswick

BRVNESVICVM — Brunswick (Germany)
BRVXELENSIS — Brussels (Brabant — Belgium)
BUENOS AYRES — Argentina
BUNDESREPUBLIK DEUTSCHLAND —
   Germany (Federal Republic)
BVILLONAEVS — Bouillon (France)
BVINA — Bonn (Germany)
BVLLON — Bouillon (France)
BVRDEQILA — Bordeaux (France)
BVRGVNDIA — Burgundy (France)

Mongolia

°BYTA HANPAMAAX MOHTOA APAYAC — Mongolia
CABILON — Chalons (Burgundy — France)
CABO VERDE — Cape Verde Islands
CAMBODGE — Cambodia
CAMERACENSIS — Cambrai (France)

Cape Verde

160

CAMEROUN — Cameroons
CAMPEN — Kampen (Netherlands)
CANTON — Switzerland
CARTIS — Chartres (France)
CATALUNA — Catalonia (Spain)
CAYENNE — French Guiana
°CCCP — Russia
CECHY A MORAVA — Bohemia and Moravia
    (Czechoslovakia)
CELE — Celles (France)
CENOHANNIS — Maine (France)
CENTRAFRICAINE — Central African Republic
CENTRO DE AMERICA — Costa Rica (mint mark CR),
    Guatemala (mint mark NG), Honduras (mint mark T)
°CEPEbPOMb — Russia
CESKOSLOVENSKA — Czechoslovakia
CHERIFIEN — Morocco
CHING KIANG — China
CHUCKRAM — Travancore (India — Native State)
CLIVIA — Cleves (France)
°CNbNPCKAR — Siberia
COCHIN CHINE FRANÇAISE — French Cochin China
    (Indo-China)
COESFELD — Koesfeld (Germany)
COLONIA — Cologne (Germany)
CONFLUENTIA — Koblenz (Trier — Germany)
CONGO BELGE — Belgian Congo
CONSTANCIA — Constance (Germany)
CORBECIA — Corvey (Germany)
CORDOBA — Argentina
COTE FRANÇAISE DES SOMALIS — French Somaliland
°CPBCKII — Serbia
°CPbHJA — Serbia
°CPbNJA — Serbia
°CTOTNHKN — Bulgaria
CUMHURIYETI — Turkey
CVGN — Cugnon (France)
DALPhS — Dauphiné (France)
DANIA — Denmark
DANMARK — Denmark
DANSK AMERIKANSK — Danish West Indies

Catalonia

Morocco

Siberia

Serbia

161

DANSKE — Denmark
DANSK VESTINDIEN — Danish West Indies
DAVANTRIA — Deventer (Netherlands)
DEMERARY & ESSEQUEBO — British Guiana
DEUTSCHE DEMOKRATISCHE REPUBLIK —
  German Democratic Republic (Eastern Zone)
DEUTSCHES REICH — Germany
DEUTSCHLAND — Germany
DEUTSCH OSTAFRIKA — German East Africa
DEUTSCH OSTAFRIKANISCHE GESELLSCHAFT —
  German East Africa Company
DEWAS — India (Native State)
D'HAITI — Haiti
DHAR — India (Native State)
D'ITALIA — Italy
DIVIONESIS — Dijon (Burgundy — France)
*DNHAPA — Yugoslavia
D.O.A. — German East Africa
DOMB — Dombes (France)
DOMINICANA — Dominican Republic
DRETMANNA — Dortmund (Germany)
*EAAADOE — Greece
*EAAHNIKH AHMOKPATIA — Greece
*EAAHNIKH ILLOAITEIA — Greece
EESTI — Estonia
EIRE — Ireland
EISTADIVM — Eichstadt (Germany)
ELVANCENSIS — Ellwangen (Germany)
EMPIRE CHERIFIEN — Morocco
EQSTRIV — Lausanne (Switzerland)
EQVITAS — Sicily (Italy)
ERFORDVM — Erfurt (Germany)
ERYTHR — Eritrea
ESPANA — Spain
ESSEQUIBO & DEMERARY — British Guiana
ESTADO DA INDIA — Portuguese India
ETABLISSEMENTS FRANÇAIS DE L'OCEANIE —
  French Oceania
ETAT FRANÇAISE — France (Vichy)
ETRVRIA — Tuscany (Italy)
EUZKADI — Viscayan Republic

Danish West Indies

Greece

Estonia

Ireland

Viscayan Republic

EYSTETTENSIS – Eichstadt (Germany)
FER — Ferrara (Italy)
FILIPINAS – Philippines
F.K. CUSTOM HOUSE – China
FLANDRIA – Flanders (Belgium)
FLORENTIA – Florence (Italy – Tuscany)
FOEDERATI BELGII – Netherlands
FOO KIEN – China

Florence

FRANÇAISE – France
FRANCOFORDIA – Frankfurt (Germany)
FRANCKISCHEN CRAIS – Franconian Circle
FRAN ET NAV – France
FREIE STADT DANZIG – Danzig (Germany)
FR ET NAV – France
FREYBURG – Fribourg (Switzerland)
FRIBVRGVM – Freiburg (Germany)
FRIDBERG – Friedberg (Germany)
FRISIA ORIENTALIS – East Friesland (Netherlands)

France

FRISING – Freising (Germany)
FUN – Korea
FUNG TIEN – China
G – Guatemala

Guatemala

GALLIARVM – Lyon (France)
GANDENSIS – Ghent (Flanders – Belgium)
GEDANENSIS – Danzig
GELRIA – Gelderland (Netherlands)
GENEVENSIS – Geneva (Switzerland)

Danzig

GENV – Genoa (Italy)
GERVNDA – Gerona (Italy)
GHANIENSIS – Ghana
GOA – Portuguese India
GOSL – Goslar (Germany)
GR (counterstamp) – Jamaica
GRAND LIBAN – Lebanon
GRAUBUNDEN – Grisons (Swiss canton)
GRIQUA TOWN – Griqualand
GRONLAND – Greenland
GUINE – Portuguese Guinea
GUINEÆ – Angola
GUINEE – Guinea
GUYANE FRANÇAISE – French Guiana

Jamaica

GVLIACVM – Jülich (Germany)
GVLICH – Jülich (Germany)
HABILITADA POR EL GOBIERNO (counterstamp) –
Costa Rica
HALAE – Hall (Germany)
HANONIE – Hainault (Belgium)
HASSIA – Hesse (Germany)
HELVETIA – Switzerland
HELVETICA – Switzerland
HERBIPOLIS – Würzburg (Germany)
HIBERNIA – Ireland
HILDES – Hildesheim (Germany)
HISPANIARUM – Spain

Spain

HISPANIARUM ET INDIARUM REX – Spanish-American
mints. Exact country of origin determined by mint mark
in legend – M (Mexico), G or NG (Guatemala), LM
or MAE (Peru), S (Santiago, Chile), PTS (Potosi,
Bolivia), P or PN or NR (Colombia)
HISPANIARUM REX – Spain
HOHENLO– Hohenlohe (Germany)
HOL – Holland (Netherlands)
HOLLANDIE – Holland (Netherlands)
HOLSATIA – Holstein (Denmark)
HO NAN – China
HOND – Honduras
HOSP ET S. SEPVL HIERVS – Malta
HRVATSKA – Croatia

Peru

HUNG SHUAN – China
HU PEH – China
HU POO – China (Empire)
HVNGARIA – Hungary
HWAN – South Korea
IEVER – Jever (Germany)

Montenegro

*ΙΙΑΡΑ – Montenegro
*ΙΙΡΗΕΤΟΡΕ – Montenegro
ILE DE LA REUNION – Reunion Island
ILES DE FRANCE ET BONAPARTE – Mauritius
INDIA PORTUGUEZA – Portuguese India
INDIE BATAV – Netherlands East Indies
INDO-CHINE FRANCAISE – French Indo-China
*IONIKON KPATOE – Ionian Islands

Ionian Islands

164

IPRA — Ypres (Netherlands)
ISLAND — Iceland
ISLES DU VENT — Windward Islands
ITALIA — Italy
IVLIACVM — Jülich (Germany)
IVNGHEIT — Aachen (Germany)
IVVAVIA — Salzburg (Austria)
*JUGOSLAVIJA — Yugoslavia
*JYPOCIIABNJE — Yugoslavia
*JYTOCNABNJA — Yugoslavia
KATANGA — Congo
*KBAXEBNHA — Montenegro
KIANG NAN — China
KIANG SEE — China
KIANG SOO — China
*KIBRIS — Cyprus
KIRIN — China
*KOIIEEK — Russia
*KONbEKb — Russia
*KPHTH — Crete
*KPHTIKH — Crete
KWANG SEA — China
KWANG TUNG — China
*KYTIPIAKH — Cyprus
L — Lima (Peru)
LATVIJAS — Latvia
LEO — Leon (Spain)
LEODIENSIS — Liège (Belgium)
LETZEBURG — Luxembourg
LIBANAISE — Lebanon
LIETUVAS — Lithuania
LIGNICIVM — Liegnitz (Germany)
LIGURE — Ligurian Republic (Italy)
LILLA — Lille (France)
LIMBVRGIE — Limburg (Germany)
LIMOVICENSIS — Limoges (France)
LINGONIS CVTS — Langres (France)
LIPSIA — Leipzig (Germany)
LIPP — Lippe (Germany)
LM — Lima (Peru)
L'OCEANIE — French Oceania

Iceland

Yugoslavia

Lithuania

Peru

165

LOMBARDO VENETO – Lombardy-Venetia (Italy)
LOTHARINGIA – Lorraine (France)
LOVANIEN – Louvain (Brabant – Belgium)
LOWENST – Löwenstein (Germany)
LUBECENSIS – Lübeck (Germany)
LUCENSIS – Lucca (Italy)
LUZERN – Lucerne (Switzerland)
LVCDVNVM – Lyon (France)
LVCENBGENSIS – Luxembourg
LVGDVNVM – Lyons (France)
LVGDVNVM BATAVORVM – Leyden
   (Netherlands)
LVNEBVRGVM – Lüneburg (Germany)
LVXEMBVRG – Luxembourg
M (on rectangular coin) – Mozambique
M – Mexico
MACUTA – Angola
MADEIRENSIS – Madeira
MAG BRIT – Great Britain
MAGYAR – Hungary
MANCHURIAN PROVINCES – China
MANTOVA – Mantua (Italy)
MARCHIE – Marche (France)
MAROC – Morocco
MECHLENB – Mecklenburg (Germany)
MEDIOLANVM – Milan (Italy)
MEGAPO – Mecklenburg (Germany)
METENSIS – Metz (Lorraine – France)
METVLLO – Melle (France)
MEXICANA – Mexico
MILETA – Malta
MIMIGARDEFORT – Münster (Germany)
MLI – Milan (Italy)
MOCAMBIQUE – Mozambique
MOGONCIA – Mainz (Germany)
°MOHETA PYbAb – Russia
MONASTER – Münster (Germany)
MONOEGI – Monaco
MUTINA – Modena (Italy)
NAMVRCEMSIS – Namur (France)
NANCEII – Nancy (Lorraine – France)

166

Lyons

Mozambique

Great Britain

Hungary

Russia

NANTIS — Nantes (Brittany — France)
°NAPA — Montenegro, Serbia
NAVARRA — Navarre (France)
NEAP — Naples (Italy)
°NEBA — Bulgaria
NEDERLANDEN — Netherlands
NEDERLANDSCH INDIE — Netherlands East Indies
NEDERLANDSE ANTILLEN — Netherlands Antilles
NEV GUINEA COMPAGNIE — German New Guinea
NG — Guatemala
NIVERSCIS — Nevers (France)
NORGE — Norway
NORIMBERGA — Nuremberg (Germany)
NORTHVSIA — Nordhausen (Germany)
NORVEG — Norway
NOUVELLE CALEDONIE — New Caledonia
NR — Nuevo Reino, Santa Fe de Bogota (Colombia)
NUEVA GRANADA — Colombia
OESTERREICH — Austria
OLOMVCEN — Olmütz (Germany)
ONCA (on rectangular coin) — Mozambique
ORANJE VRYS STAAT — Orange Free State (Orange
    River Colony)
OSNABRVGA — Osnabrück (Germany)
OSTAFRIKANISCHE — German East Africa
OSTERREICH — Austria
PADERB — Paderborn (Germany)
PAPIA — Pavia (Italy)
PARMAE — Parma (Italy)
PASSANIA — Passau (Germany)
PECUNIA INSULANA — Azores
PECUNIA MADEIRESIS — Madeira
PEI YANG — China
PENNIA — Finland
PFALZ — Palatinate (Germany)
PICTAVIENTSIS — Poitou (France)
P.M. (counterstamped) — Mozambique
POLSKA — Poland
POLSKIE — Poland
PONTISIENSI — Pontoise (France)
PONTIV — Ponthien (France)

Bulgaria

Colombia

Austria

Poland

PONT MAX — Papal States or Vatican City
PORTUGALIÆ — Portugal
PORTUGUESA — Portugal
POTOSI — Bolivia
PREUSSEN — Prussia (Germany)
PROCENIE — Forcalquier (France)
POVINCIA — Provence (France)
PROVINCIAS DEL RIO DE LA PLATA — Argentina

Papal States

PTS (superimposed on one another) — Bolivia
°PYbAb — Russia
QUETZAL — Guatemala
QUINDAR — Albania
QVOCVNQVE IECERIS STABIT — Isle of Man
RATISBON — Regensburg (Germany)
REDONIS — Rennes (France)
REGNUM ITALICUM — Eritrea
REMIS — Reims (France)
RENAV — Château-Renaud (France)
REP CENTRAFRICAINE — Central African Republic
REPUBLIQUE FRANÇAISE — France or colonies
REPUBLICA PORTUGUESA — Portugal or colonies
R.F. — France
RIGSBANK — Denmark
RIO DE LA PLATA — Argentina
RODES — Rovergue (France)
ROMANA — Rumania
ROMANIA — Rumania
ROMANIEI — Rumania
ROMANILOR — Rumania
ROM IMP — Holy Roman Emperor (Austria)
RUANDA URUNDI — Belgian Congo
S — Santiago (Chile)
SAARLAND — Saar
SABAUD — Savoy (Italy)
SABAVADI — Savoy (Italy)
SACHSEN — Saxony (Germany)
SAILANA — India (Native State)
SALISBVRGVM — Salzburg (Austria)
SALVTIARVM — Carmagnola (Italy)
SAORSTAT EIREANN — Ireland
SARDEGNA — Sardinia (Italy)

Bolivia

Château Renaud

Chile

168

SAXONIA — Saxony (Germany)
SCHLESIEN — Silesia
SCHLESW-HOLST — Schleswig and Holstein (Denmark)
SCHWEIZER — Switzerland
SCI DIONYSIM — St. Denis (France)
SCOTORVM — Scotland
SEDE VACANTE — Papal States or Vatican City
SHANG TUNG — China
SHQIPERI — Albania
SHQIPNI — Albania
SHQIPTAREVET — Albania
SICILIAE ET HIERVSALEM — Naples and Sicily
SILESIAE — Silesia (Austria)
SLOVENSKA — Slovakia (Czechoslovakia)
SLOVENSKYCH — Slovakia (Czechoslovakia)
S.M. — Sweden
S. MARINI — San Marino
S. MARINO — San Marino
SOMALIA ITALIANA — Italian Somaliland
SOMALIS — French Somaliland
SOMMER ISLANDS — Bermuda
SOSATVM — Soest (Germany)
S. TOME E PRINCIPE — St. Thomas and Prince Islands
STYRELSE GRONLAND — Greenland
STYRIAE — Styria (Austria)
SUD — Mexico (Revolutionary)
SUID AFRIKA — South Africa
SUOMEN — Finland
SUOMI — Finland
SURINAME — Surinam
SVECIAE — Sweden
SVERIGES — Sweden
SVESSIONIS — Soissons (France)
SYRIE — Syria
SZE CHUEN — China
TAI CH'ING TI KUO — China (Empire)
TAI WAN — China
TASAVALTA — Finland
TAZHTAIE — Ionian Islands
THEROTMANNI — Dortmund (Germany)
TICINUM — Pavia (Italy)

Saxony

Sicily

Sweden

Sweden

TIGVRINAE – Zürich (Switzerland)
TIROL – Tyrol (Austria)
TOKYO – Japan
TOLETO – Toledo (Spain)
TOLOSA – Toulouse (France)
TORNACVM – Tournai (Netherlands)
TOSCANA – Tuscany (Italy)
TRAIECTVM – Utrecht (Netherlands)
TRAJECTVM AD MOSAM – Maastricht
   (Netherlands)
TRANSISVLANIA – Overijssel (Netherlands)
TRANSYL – Transylvania (Austria)
TRAVANCORE – India (Native State)
TRECAS – Troyes (Champagne – France)
TREMONIA – Dortmund (Germany)
TREVERIS – Trier
TSINGKIANG – China
TUNISIE – Tunisia
TURKIYE – Turkey
TVCIVM – Deutz (Cologne – Germany)
TVLLV – Taul (Lorraine – France)
TVRENA – Turenne (France)
TVRICVM – Zürich (Switzerland)
TVRINGIA – Thuringia (Germany)
TVRONVS – Tours (France)
TVVCIVM – Deutz (Cologne – Germany)
TYR – Tyrol (Austria)
*UPHETOPE – Montenegro
UPPER CANADA – Ontario (Canada)
VABARIIK – Estonia
VALENCERENSIS – Valenciennes
   (Burgundy – France)
VALENTIAI – Valence (France)
VALLS D'ANDORRA – Andorra
VATICANO – Vatican City
VEDOME – Vendôme (France)
VENASINI – Avignon (France)
VENECIAS – Venice (Italy)
VENETVS – Venice (Italy)
VENT – Windward Islands
VERDA – Werden (Germany)

Utrecht

Overijssel

Venice

170

VESTINDIEN – Danish West Indies
VIGO – Great Britain
VINDELICORVM – Augsburg (Germany)
VINDOBONA – Vienna (Italy)
VIRDVNCM – Verdun (Lorraine – France)
VIROMENDI – Vermandois (France)
VNGARIE — Hungary
WERDINVM – Werden (Germany)
WESTFRI – West Frisia (Netherlands)
WESTPHALEN – Westphalia (Germany)
WON – Korea
WRATISLAVIA – Breslau (Germany)
WURTEM – Württemberg (Germany)
YANG – Korea
YEN – Japan
YUN NAN – China
ZAR – South African Republic
ZEELANDIA – Zeeland (Netherlands)
ZEL – Zeeland (Netherlands)
ZUID AFRIKA – South Africa
ZUID AFRIKAANSCHE REPUBLIEK –
    South African Republic

Great Britain

Hungary

West Frisia

South African Republic

171

VISUAL IDENTIFICATION

Coins without legends or with inscriptions that are in Arabic or other languages not similar to English can be attributed by comparing them with the pictures in this section to locate a coin of similar type.

Afghanistan
(mosque)

Burma
(lion)

Ceylon
(lion)

China
(dragon)

Comoro Islands
(weapons)

Egypt
(fez)

Egypt-U.A.R.
(eagle)

Ethiopia
(lion)

India
(Asoka pillar)

Iran-Persia
(lion)

Iraq
(grain)

Israel
(Hebrew inscription)

Japan
(chrysanthemum)

Korea
(flower)

Libya
(coat of arms)

Maldive Islands
(crossed flags)

Manchukuo
(lotus flower)

Mongolia
(emblem)

Morocco
(star)

Muscat & Oman
(crossed daggers)

Nepal
(trident)

Pakistan
(crescent)

Saudi Arabia
(palm)

174

Sudan
(camel)

Syria
(eagle)

Thailand-Siam
(coat of arms)

Tibet
(design)

Thailand-Siam
(elephant)

Turkey
(toughra)

Tunisia (Arabic inscription, tree)

Yemen
(branch)

Zanzibar
(scales)

Collecting Gold Coins

Since the earliest periods of recorded history, gold has had an allure for the human race. Its warm color and brilliant luster have an irresistible attraction. Gold's softness makes the metal easy to work, yet it is virtually indestructible. Gold does not corrode, rust or tarnish. Even acid has no effect on it. Gold is just rare enough—there is enough so that small quantities are within the reach of nearly everyone; rare enough to make it an object of value.

The great ancient civilizations, including the Egyptians, Assyrians and Etruscans, treasured ornaments and jewels fashioned from gold. Egyptian tombs have yielded gold statuettes and elaborate ornaments. The pharaoh Tutankhamen (r. 1357-51 B.C.) was buried in a solid gold coffin weighing more than one ton! Gold's first use as money was not in the form of coins but as a unit of weight, the shekel, which was about one quarter of an ounce or the value of a healthy ox.

The first use of gold in coinage came in Lydia, a kingdom in Asia Minor, along what is now the Aegean coast of Turkey. Lydia was at the head of the caravan routes to India and had access by sea to all of the lands bordering the Mediterranean. The Lydian kings were fabulously rich, both from commerce and abundant natural deposits of gold and silver.

About 650 B.C. during the reign of King Ardys (652-615 B.C.), the Lydians hit upon the idea of shaping precious metal into convenient-sized pieces of fixed weight and purity. These first crude lumps were punchmarked by individual merchants to enable them to recognize pieces they had previously weighed and tested.

The first large-scale issue of gold coins occurred under King Croesus (560-546 B.C.) whose name we still use today as a standard of comparison for great wealth. Croesus' coins show the facing heads of a lion and a bull, symbols of royal power. The reverse had just the simple indentation of a rectangular punch. The coins are called staters which means "weigher" or norm of value.

Pure gold stater issued by King Croesus of Lydia, 560-546 B.C.

The Lydian Empire was toppled by Cyrus of Persia in 546 B.C., and his successor, Darius the Great (521-486 B.C.) struck enormous quantities of a gold coin called the daric. One gold daric is believed to have been a month's pay for a Persian soldier. Darius used nearly pure gold for his coinage but experience had shown that the addition of a small amount of base metal resulted in harder, longer-lasting coins. In spite of the huge mintages of these early coins, not many have come down to us as they were melted and recoined by subsequent conquerors.

Gold daric of Persia struck under Darius the Great, 521-486 B.C.

In ancient Greece and its colonies, coinage was considered a right of the individual city-states. While many of them produced an extensive coinage in silver, gold was generally held in temple treasuries and minted only in cases of extreme necessity. Only after the Macedonians came to power under Philip II (359-336 B.C.) and Alexander the Great (356-323 B.C.) was Greece provided with an abundant gold coinage. The basic gold coin of the Macedonian Empire was again the stater, often called a philippus, struck in 23 carat gold. These staters circulated to the farthest reaches of the then-known world where they were eventually imitated by local minters as far away as ancient Britain.

Macedonian gold stater of Alexander the Great, 356-323 B.C.

The Romans, too, had an extensive gold coinage beginning in 215 B.C. The basic denomination was the aureus, the Latin word for golden. Roman gold coins provide us with a portrait gallery of the emperors over the centuries. Various members of imperial families including wives, adopted heirs, daughters, sons, brothers, sisters, mothers, even in one case a grandmother, were portrayed on Roman coins. The gold aureus endured until the time of Constantine the Great (307-337 A.D.) who replaced it with a gold coin called the solidus.

The aureus was the standard gold coin of the Roman Empire. These specimens carry the portraits of Antoninus Pius, 138-161, and his wife Faustina.

Constantine the Great transferred his court from Rome to Byzantium, establishing a new empire that was Greek in language and custom yet Roman by tradition and heritage. The gold pieces of this empire were kept absolutely stable for eight centuries and they circulated throughout Europe where they were known as bezants. In the absence of adequate Western coinage, the bezant became the unquestioned standard of value and money of account throughout the Middle Ages.

This solidus of Nicephorus II, 963-969, shows a portrait of Christ on the obverse, the Virgin Mary and the emperor on the reverse.

The Crusades sent gold flowing back to Europe in exchange for goods and as spoils of war. By the late 13th century, Venice had become Europe's richest city while Florence, with more than 100 banking houses, had become the world's financial hub. Both cities acquired large supplies of gold and began minting their own coins. The standard-size coin, called a ducat in Venice, was given different names in different localities, the name often being taken from the design; for instance, the gold coin of Florence was known as the "fiorino d'oro," Italian for "little

First issued during the 13th century, the florin of Florence (left) and the ducat of Venice (right) set the standard for several centuries.

flower of gold," an allusion to the lily emblem on the reverse. Similarly, there are leopards, angels, nobles and sovereigns from England, aguels (lambs), ecus (shields), and couronnes (crowns) from France, and guldens (goldens) from Germany.

The quest for gold led explorers to the far corners of the earth. The discovery of the Americas started a river of gold flowing back to Europe. The invention of rolling mills for producing metal sheets of standard thickness, punches for stamping out uniformly round planchets, and screw presses for impressing the design onto blank planchets greatly improved and speeded up the production of gold coins. From this point until well into the 20th century, gold coins were minted by almost every government and petty state.

This 1757 gold 8 escudo coin from the Mexico City mint is of the type popularly known in North America as a gold doubloon.

A listing of just the types and denominations issued during these centuries is enough to fill a large-size catalogue. The greatest age of gold coinage, however, was the hundred-year period between the downfall of Napoleon and the start of World War I. Rich gold strikes were made during those years, the world was comparatively peaceful, commerce flourished, and gold coins were in circulation nearly everywhere.

At the outbreak of World War I, governments stopped minting gold coins in order to preserve their stocks of precious metal. Citizens on both sides, as in all previous wars, hoarded gold coins, certain of their intrinsic value if nothing else. Paper money filled the void. When the war ended, paper currency had been accepted and, even when the paper notes were again exchangeable for gold coins, there was no great rush to convert them. Most nations never resumed striking regular issue gold coins. In countries where gold was minted, the public used the coins mostly for birthday presents and holiday gifts. A few countries also produced limited issues of gold coins as commemoratives. Another group of nations—those newly created or newly independent—felt the need to issue gold coins as a mark of their sovereignty.

Stock market crashes, bank failures and economic depression around the world forced Great Britain to suspend gold sales in 1931, and in 1933 the minting of gold coins came to an end in the U.S. as well. Banks were prohibited from paying out gold and outstanding coins were confiscated by making it compulsory to turn them in to the U.S. Treasury. Gold bullion was revalued upwards from $20.67 to $35 an ounce. The official price was held at this level until 1968. Gold is now traded freely in the international market with ever-changing daily quotations.

The Gold Order of 1933 did allow collectors and dealers to hold and exchange gold coins of recognized numismatic value. New interpretations and amendments were issued beginning in 1954 until finally all restrictions on ownership of gold were removed as of January, 1975. U.S. citizens may now buy, sell or hold gold in any form.

Collecting gold coins has long been the highest peak of the numismatic hobby. While all gold coins have a readily determined intrinsic value, they also command a greater or lesser premium above their worth as bullion depending upon the rarity of the particular coin and the demand for it. Well-chosen, attractive gold coins of historic interest seem to increase in value steadily as the demand for them grows. Any one of them is an object that you can enjoy

Commemorative coins struck in limited quantity have long been appreciated by collectors for their investment value as well as their historic significance. This Austrian 100 corona piece of 1908 marks the 60th year of Emperor Franz Joseph's reign. The total mintage was 16,026 coins, each valued today at more than $1,500.

owning over the years. To be a successful investor in gold coins of recognized numismatic value does involve considerable reading and study. Not only must you know what you are buying but you must be able to accurately predict the future trends of numismatic enthusiasms—which coins or series are likely to be more in demand in the years ahead than they are right now. Generally, the best investments are coins with historic significance or with a good story behind them. The poorest investments are often coins that are being heavily advertised at the moment and likely to be forgotten once the issue is sold out.

With the end of the restrictions on gold ownership, however, many people have shown an interest in coins less for their historic worth than for their intrinsic value. If you are interested in buying gold as a store of value, a measure against the erosion of your savings by inflation, then there is certainly more pleasure in a collection of fine gold coins than in a plain bar of metal. Certain coins have come to be recognized as having a high intrinsic value in relation to their market price. Chief among these are the coins that follow, listed with their fineness and the weight in troy ounces of the amount of pure gold contained in each. To determine the intrinsic value of a coin at any given market price for gold, you need only multiply the weight given by the prevailing price. The weight and value of fractions or multiples of a given unit are always in exact proportion to the basic coin.

Both of these issues have been officially restruck in recent years.

Country	Denomination	Fineness	Weight	Gold Weight
Austria	4 Ducats	.986 fine	14.0000 oz.	.4438 oz.
	20 Corona	.900	6.7750	.1960

| Belgium | 20 Francs | .900 | 6.4516 | .1867 |

| Chile | 100 Pesos | .900 | 20.3397 | .5885 |

| Colombia | 5 Pesos | .916⅔ | 7.9881 | .2354 |
| Cuba | 5 Pesos | .900 | 8.3592 | .2419 |

| Denmark | 20 Kroner | .900 | 8.9606 | .2593 |

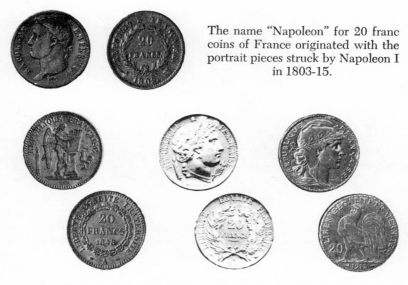

The name "Napoleon" for 20 franc coins of France originated with the portrait pieces struck by Napoleon I in 1803-15.

All of these French designs were struck in large quantities.

France   20 Francs   .900   6.4516   .1867

Under the German Empire, 24 different cities and states had their own gold coinage. Coins such as these from Hamburg and Prussia were struck in large quantity but some other issues are very rare.

Germany   20 Marks   .900   7.9650   .23046

During Queen Victoria's long reign, coins were issued with three different portraits. Dealers offer these as young, jubilee and old heads.

Great Britain   1 Pound   .916⅔   7.9881   .2354

This coin has been officially restruck in recent years.

Hungary   20 Korona   .900   6.7750   .1960

Italy   20 Lire   .900   6.4516   .1867

Mexico	50 Pesos	.900	41.6666	1.2056
	20 Pesos	.900	16.6666	.4823
	10 Pesos	.900	8.3333	.2411
	5 Pesos	.900	4.1666	.1206
	2½ Pesos	.900	2.0833	.0603
	2 Pesos	.900	1.6666	.0482

Between 1892 and 1933, Queen Wilhelmina's coins showed her as a young girl, a young woman, an adult, and a mature woman.

Netherlands   10 Guilders   .900   6.7290   .1947

Netherlands
East Indies   1 Ducat   .986   3.5000   .1109

Russia   10 Roubles   .900   8.6026   .2489

South Africa   1 Krugerrand   .916⅔   33.9305   1.000

Sweden   20 Kronor   .900   8.9606   .2593

Switzerland   20 Francs   .900   6.4516   .1867

Turkey   100 Piastres   .916⅔   7.2166   .2127

For the designs of later issues, see pages 52 and 53.

U.S.A.				
	20 Dollars	.900	33.4370	.9675
	10 Dollars	.900	16.7185	.4838
	5 Dollars	.900	8.3592	.2419
	2½ Dollars	.900	4.1796	.1209

Examples of many of the above coins are available to careful shoppers at a price less than double their intrinsic gold value. All were struck in large enough quantity to be readily available in extremely fine or even mint uncirculated condition. Gold coins in superior condition are readily resold.

190

Many recent issues of gold coins have been minted by private firms under authorization from various governments. Some of these coins fit into established coinage systems, others are denominations never used in the coun-

Though no gold coins are now struck for circulation, many modern gold issues are related to the established currency system of their issuing countries and their designs refer to events of national significance. Other issues are of questionable merit. This 100 balboa coin of Panama carries a portrait of the nation's discoverer. This 100 gourde coin of Haiti shows a portrait of the American Indian, Chief Sitting Bull.

tries before and the designs often have nothing to do with the history or culture of the issuing nations. Despite their legal tender status, these pieces are more like medals and it is unlikely that their value will increase at the same rate as genuine coins.

Since even the commonest gold coins represent the investment of a fair number of dollars, choose carefully and, above all, make your purchases from a reputable dealer. Be sure to keep your coins in a safe place, preferably a safe-deposit box.

INDEX